Low-Carb Diet *for Beginners*

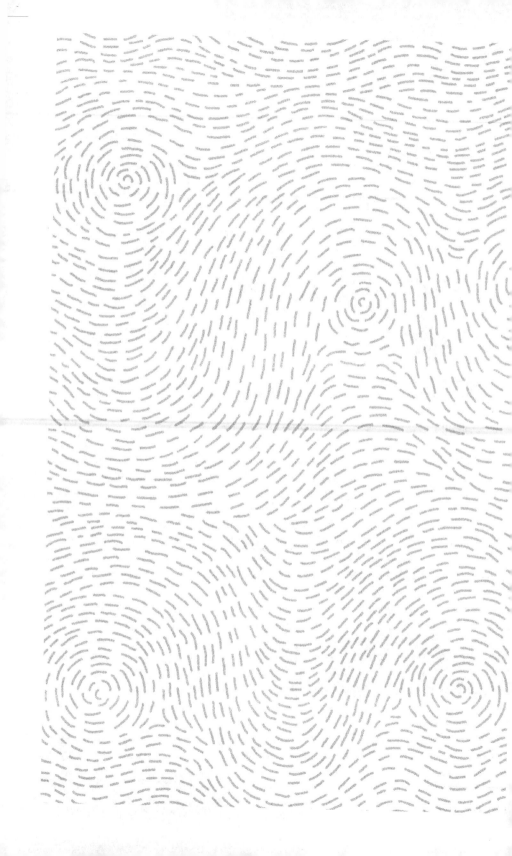

Low-Carb Diet
for Beginners

ESSENTIAL LOW-CARB RECIPES
TO START LOSING WEIGHT

MENDOCINO PRESS

Contents

Introduction   1

PART ONE

The Low-Carb Diet

Chapter One: What Is a Low-Carb Diet?   5
How and Why Low-Carb Diets Work   6
Why Choose a Low-Carb Diet for Weight Loss?   8
How to Lose Weight on a Low-Carb Diet   9
Health Benefits of Low-Carb Eating   11
Debunking Common Myths About Low-Carb Diets   12

Chapter Two: Getting Started with the Low-Carb Diet   15
How Much Carbohydrate Is Enough?   15
Eliminate the Bad Carbs   17
What About Good Carbs?   17
Okay, Sugar's Out. What About Artificial Sweeteners?   17
Good Fats Versus Bad Fats   18
Alcoholic Beverages   20
Putting It All Together   20
Low-Carb Shopping Tips   21
Stocking the Low-Carb Kitchen   21
Tips for Dining Out   22
Cooking Tips   22
Ten Tips for Success   24

Chapter Three: The Meal Plan   27
How to Use This Low-Carb Diet Meal Plan   27
Seven-Day Meal Plan   29

PART TWO

Recipes

Chapter Four: Breakfast 33

Chapter Five: Appetizers and Snacks 51

Chapter Six: Soups and Salads 63

Chapter Seven: Entrées 81

Chapter Eight: Desserts 97

Appendix A: Ten Tips for Dining Out 113

Appendix B: High-Carb Foods and Lower-Carb Alternatives 115

Appendix C: Low-Carb Foods 116

Index 118

Introduction

W elcome to *Low-Carb Diet for Beginners*. It's more than likely that you've picked up this book because you want to lose weight. As you'll learn here, many people successfully lose weight by reducing the carbohydrates in their diets. Low-carb diets also have many other health benefits, including:

- Alleviating depression
- Increasing energy
- Improving cholesterol levels
- Reducing insulin resistance
- Preventing diabetes

Low-carb diets have become extremely popular in recent years for the simple reason that they are easy to follow and are a quick and relatively painless solution to many health issues, including excess weight, sluggishness and fatigue, and poor mood. Sticking to a low-carb diet can help you conquer sugar cravings, and it can regulate your blood sugar and certain hormones that control appetite and satiety. As a result, you'll lose weight, decrease your blood pressure, reduce your risk of diabetes and other diseases, increase your energy, and boost your mood.

In most low-carb diets, there are no restrictions on portion size, or on amounts of calories, fat, sodium, or cholesterol you consume. For this reason, low-carb diets are very appealing to those who enjoy eating and aren't inclined to painstakingly count the calories of everything they eat throughout the day. A low-carb diet requires restricting only the amount of carbohydrates you eat, with per-day carbohydrate limits ranging from 50 to 100 grams, depending on your size, activity level, and other factors. Refined grains and added sugars are entirely off the menu, but many other foods can be enjoyed virtually without a care.

Whether you've tried a low-carb diet before or this is the first time you've given it any thought at all, you might think that you'll have to give up all the foods you love most. Happily, this book will show you that's not true. In fact, many of your favorite foods can still be on your menu.

If you are trying to lose a few (or many) pounds, control your blood sugar, reduce your blood pressure, have more energy, reduce cravings, or alleviate symptoms of depression, a low-carb diet may very well be the answer you've been looking for.

Low-Carb Diet for Beginners is filled with information that will help you tackle these issues and more. You will find all of the basic information you need to better understand low-carb eating and to learn how to make changes in your eating habits. This book provides:

- An introduction to low-carb diets, how and why they work, and the truth about many common low-carb diet myths
- A basic low-carb eating plan
- Numerous easy, quick, and delicious recipes that fit the plan

The book is divided into two parts. Part One provides an overview of low-carb diets, a detailed explanation of the science behind low-carb eating and how it affects your weight and general health, and an examination of the health benefits of low-carb eating. It also provides a guide to getting started with low-carb eating, and offers tips for reading nutrition labels, grocery shopping, stocking your pantry, and low-carb cooking. It answers many commonly asked questions about low-carb diets, debunks common myths about low-carb diets, and explains the difference between "good carbs" and "bad carbs." Finally, a seven-day meal plan shows you what low-carb eating looks like on a day-to-day basis.

Part Two offers low-carb recipes that will help you to make quick and simple meals that are very low in carbs but full of delicious flavor. With these recipes in hand, you'll begin your low-carb diet by eating meals that truly satisfy you. Since you'll be eating foods you love and are enjoying your meals, you'll be more likely to stick to the diet for the long term. Before you know it, you'll be well on your way to better health.

PART ONE

The Low-Carb Diet

CHAPTER ONE WHAT IS A LOW-CARB DIET?

CHAPTER TWO GETTING STARTED WITH THE LOW-CARB DIET

CHAPTER THREE THE MEAL PLAN

CHAPTER 1

What Is a Low-Carb Diet?

A low-carbohydrate diet is any diet plan in which carbohydrates are limited. Carbohydrates, often called carbs, are nutrient compounds found in a wide variety of foods—both healthful and unhealthful—including bread, legumes, dairy products, potatoes, broccoli, apples, pasta, soda, corn, and chocolate. The most common forms of carbohydrates are sugar, fiber, and starch.

The quantity of carbohydrates a person can eat on a low-carb diet varies widely from person to person. The goal is to find a level that works for you, the level where you lose weight and feel great. For most people, carbs will be about 20 percent (or less) of their daily caloric intake. For the average 2,000-calorie-per-day diet, that means about 100 grams of carbohydrates are allowed per day. In most low-carbohydrate diets, refined grains (white flour, white rice, etc.) and added sugars are considered mostly, if not entirely, off limits.

There are many different low-carb diet plans, including Atkins, the Zone Diet, Protein Power, Sugar Busters, South Beach, the Paleo or Caveman Diet, and many others. While these diets all differ from one another, the one thing they have in common is that they severely restrict dietary carbohydrates and rely on protein and fats for the majority of daily calories.

Low-carbohydrate diets are extremely popular among those trying to lose weight. Many people who embark on low-carb diets report that their energy levels soar as their cravings for carb-heavy foods plummet. These diets are fairly easy to follow since they do not require detailed tracking of foods or calories eaten. And many people lose a significant amount of weight on these diets, adding greatly to their appeal.

HOW AND WHY LOW-CARB DIETS WORK

At the most basic level, all weight-loss diets work by reducing your overall caloric intake to below the level that your body uses throughout the day, creating what's known as a calorie deficit (consuming fewer calories than you burn). Many diets help you to lose weight simply by restricting the number of calories you consume each day so that you create a calorie deficit. This is how low-calorie diets work. It is also how low-fat diets work. Because fat has more calories per gram than either carbohydrates or protein, by reducing the amount of fat you eat, you reduce your calorie intake.

It may come as a surprise to you that the low-carb diets cause weight loss in the same way, by creating a calorie deficit. The difference is that low-carb diets work not by telling you how many calories you can put in your mouth, but by affecting your body's internal engine—the hormones and neurotransmitters that determine your hunger, satiety, energy levels, and cravings—and thereby causing you to want fewer calories. Numerous scientific studies, in fact, have shown that people lose about the same amount of weight on a low-carb diet as on a low-calorie diet, even though they do not limit portions or count calories. People on low-carb diets, it seems, have fewer cravings and feel satisfied with fewer calories. As a result, they naturally consume fewer calories, and therefore they lose weight.

To understand how and why the low-carb diet works, we first have to look at what happens to carbohydrates after you consume them. The human body's primary fuel source is carbohydrates. After eating carbohydrates, through the process of digestion your body breaks them down into simple sugars, which are then absorbed into the bloodstream, where they are known as blood sugar (glucose). With the help of insulin, glucose is carried to your body's cells, where it is used for energy, the fuel for everything you do, from breathing or walking to running a marathon. Excess glucose is converted to fat. When carbohydrates are limited, the body is forced to burn the stores of glucose in the fat cells for energy. On a most basic level, then, low-carbohydrate diets work by limiting the body's fuel and forcing it to burn its fat stores for energy.

But there is more to it than that. Insulin's job is to take glucose, or sugar, from your blood and deliver it to the fat cells. The problem is that when insulin sends those glucose calories to your fat cells, you no longer have access to those calories for energy. Your blood sugar plummets and you feel lousy—lethargic and hungry. So your body responds by eating more to make up for the loss of energy, which sends more glucose to your fat cells, which causes you to eat even more.

Put all this together and you see that when your body produces excess insulin, the calories you consume turn directly into fat, and yet your body feels as if it is starving. As a result, you eat more, which only creates more fat.

Where does the excess insulin come from to begin with? Research shows that it comes from eating a diet high in carbs, especially refined grains and added sugar. This high-carb diet increases your body's production of insulin, which creates a biochemical drive to eat more and burn less energy.

Meanwhile, two other bodily hormones, leptin and ghrelin, are designed to help regulate your appetite, telling the brain when you are hungry or satiated. Unfortunately, when you are overweight, both those hormones don't function properly.

Let's look at leptin first. Leptin is secreted primarily in fat cells, and it signals the brain when you have consumed enough fuel, conveying that you are satisfied and that you have the energy you need to go about your business. Because leptin is secreted by fat cells, the more fat you have, the more leptin you produce. And since leptin decreases appetite, increased leptin should help you to lose weight. But this is not the case in people who are overweight. So what's going on?

It is true that the more fat you have, the more leptin your body produces. In theory, the more the leptin you produce, the less hungry you should be and the less food you should eat. And the less fat your body has, the less leptin you should produce, which should make you hungrier and cause you to eat more.

People who are obese do, in fact, have very high levels of leptin. You'd think that would mean that those people would automatically eat only the number of calories that they need, and yet they continue to gain weight. Why is that? It turns out that insulin blocks leptin at the brain, preventing it from delivering its message of satiety. This is called leptin resistance—when leptin is unable to do its job because of high levels of insulin. So the person eats more, which produces more insulin, which creates more fat. You see where this is going, right?

In contrast to leptin, ghrelin, which is produced primarily in the stomach, tells your brain when you are hungry. Ghrelin levels go up when you haven't eaten for a while or when you are limiting your calories. Most of the time, ghrelin and leptin work together in a fine balance. As one increases, the other decreases to keep your appetite under control. If your body is in balance, when you haven't eaten in a while, your ghrelin level rises and tells your brain that you are hungry. You eat a meal and your leptin level rises, telling your brain that you are full and that your stomach can stop producing ghrelin. But if you have developed leptin resistance, this harmony is disrupted. Your brain doesn't get the signal that you are full and so you feel an overwhelming urge to keep eating.

Some of the common recommendations for maintaining a balance between leptin and ghrelin include: eating sufficient calories to keep your body from going into starvation mode, eating plenty of protein, not skipping meals, avoiding fructose, and increasing consumption of healthy fats. It's no coincidence that all of these recommendations are consistent with a low-carb diet.

The bottom line is that overeating carbohydrates can lead to increased insulin levels, which prevents calories from being used for energy and causes more glucose to be stored as fat, which leads to leptin resistance, excessive ghrelin levels, and overeating.

The low-carb diet, then, works by lowering insulin levels, which causes the body to burn both glucose and stored fat for energy while allowing leptin to deliver its message of satiety to the brain, restoring the balance between leptin and ghrelin. Ultimately this helps you shed excess weight and reduce risk factors for a variety of health conditions.

WHY CHOOSE A LOW-CARB DIET FOR WEIGHT LOSS?

The quickest answer to that question is: Because it works. And this isn't just some newfangled fad, either. Remember how your mom—or grandma, as the case may be—always used to ignore the bread basket and skip dessert when she wanted to slim down a bit? In fact, since as early as the mid-1800s, doctors and scientists have been uncovering ample evidence of the effectiveness of weight-loss diets that limit refined and simple carbohydrates.

The idea of restricting consumption of carbohydrates to lose weight was first popularized by a formerly obese English undertaker named William Banting. Banting's self-published booklet, *Letter on Corpulence, Addressed to the Public*, detailed the low-carb diet—four meals a day consisting of meat, greens, fruits, and dry wine—that had helped him slim down after many other diets had failed him. He emphasized avoiding sugar, starch, beer, milk, and butter.

Sure, you can lose weight on any diet as long as you create a calorie deficit, but there are a couple of problems with the straight calorie-restriction approach.

The first and most obvious problem is hunger. When people simply cut calories, they feel hungry. And no one likes to feel hungry, even if it's just for a few days (or hours!) and especially if it's a long-term situation. No matter how much a person wants to lose weight, they will eventually give in to hunger, which leads to the yo-yo effect, where you lose weight only to gain it back again, and then try to lose it again, in a continuing cycle.

Thanks to biochemical reactions, low-carbohydrate diets have a distinct advantage over those that simply restrict calories. As we have learned, by restricting carbs, you lower your body's production of insulin, which allows more of the glucose in your blood to be burned for energy instead of being stored as fat, and allows leptin to do its job of signaling the brain when you have eaten a sufficient amount. In other words, you feel satisfied with less food. Eating simple carbohydrates, on the other hand, increases your appetite. So even though low-carb dieters aren't actively counting calories, they end up eating fewer of them simply because they feel less hungry.

Recent studies have shown that people who restrict their carbohydrate intake not only eat fewer calories, but actually burn more calories even while at rest than people who eat high-carbohydrate diets. So a low-carb diet may increase your metabolism while at the same time reducing your hunger, making it easier for you to eat less and burn more.

HOW TO LOSE WEIGHT ON A LOW-CARB DIET

To be successful on a low-carb diet, it is important to first understand a bit about carbohydrates, which foods contain them, and the difference between simple carbohydrates ("bad carbs") and complex carbohydrates ("good carbs"). Although carbohydrates have gotten a bad rap in recent years, some are, in fact, crucial for good health.

Good Carbs Versus Bad Carbs

There are two types of carbohydrates: Simple carbohydrates and complex carbohydrates. Simple carbohydrates are the so-called bad ones.

The primary difference between the good carbs and bad carbs is fiber. The digestive system breaks all carbohydrates down into sugar (glucose), which is the body's source of energy. Carbohydrates that contain very little fiber break down much more quickly than those that contain a lot of fiber. The quicker glucose hits your bloodstream, the more severe the resulting spike in blood sugar will be.

Good carbs, or complex carbohydrates, are those that are full of fiber and nutrients. Because of their higher fiber content, complex carbohydrates are absorbed slowly into our systems, thereby not causing the extreme spikes in blood sugar levels that lead to overproduction of insulin and leptin resistance. Good carbs serve as easily accessible energy for the body, contain lots of important nutrients, and are the body's only source of fiber.

Complex carbohydrates are plant foods that are minimally refined—such as vegetables, fruits, beans, and whole grains—and are full of nutrients as well as fiber, which, while it is not digested, provides all sorts of health benefits. Fiber slows down the absorption of other nutrients eaten at the same meal, including carbohydrates, preventing blood sugar spikes, hence preventing spikes in insulin production and leptin resistance. Fiber also has the added benefit of helping you feel full with fewer calories and for a longer period of time. Whole grains, beans, vegetables, and fruits are all examples of good carbs.

Good carbs are found in:

- Nonstarchy vegetables (leafy greens, broccoli, cauliflower, zucchini, cucumbers)
- Beans and other legumes (black beans, pinto beans, peanuts)
- Whole grains (brown rice, oats, millet, bulgur)
- Nonstarchy fruits (berries, melons, apples, grapes, peaches, nectarines)

Simple carbohydrates are plant foods that have been highly refined and stripped of their beneficial fiber and nutrients, or those that are naturally de- void of fiber and nutrients. These include refined sugar (including corn syrup and other caloric sweeteners) and grains like white flour and white rice. White potatoes, certain other starchy vegetables, and some fruits fall into this category as well, since they are high in natural sugars and starch but low in other nutrients and fiber. Many of these foods provide next to nothing in the way of nutrients. They are empty calories that cause blood sugar to spike, setting off the vicious insulin-fat-storage–leptin-resistance cycle that leads to weight gain.

Bad carbs are found in:

- White flour
- White bread
- White rice
- White potatoes
- Added sugar

While simple carbs may provide quick energy for the body, that energy is wasted if you are not using it to run a race or participate in some other demanding physical activity.

The most effective low-carb diets are those that eliminate simple carbs altogether, while limiting carbohydrates from complex carbs to a level that provides the needed dietary fiber and nutrients but does not create extreme spikes in blood sugar.

Low-Carb Diet for Beginners focuses on severely restricting or eliminating bad carbs from the diet and choosing good carbs in moderate quantities in order to reap the benefits of the nutrients, fiber, and energy they provide.

HEALTH BENEFITS OF LOW-CARB EATING

Low-carb diets have many health benefits. The first and most obvious one is weight loss. Being overweight or obese is associated with an increased risk for the development of a host of diseases, including cancer, diabetes, and heart disease. Reducing your weight by as little as 7 to 10 percent can reverse or prevent diabetes, lower your blood pressure, cholesterol, and triglyceride levels, and help you sleep better.

A few other health benefits of low-carb diets include lower blood sugar levels, which can significantly lower your risk of developing cancer, diabetes, heart disease, and dementia. Stabilizing your blood sugar level also makes you feel better and more energetic, and reduces cravings.

Five signs that your blood sugar is too high: Thirst, frequent illness, fatigue, frequent yeast infections (vaginal, rashes in other moist areas of the body, or athlete's foot), and frequent hunger.

Low-carb eating can also significantly lower insulin levels and reduce insulin resistance, both of which are significant risk factors for cardiovascular disease. Low-carb eating has also been shown to help lower blood pressure, which is one of the strongest risk factors for heart disease and stroke.

Additionally, a low-carb diet can lower blood levels of triglycerides and raise HDL (good) cholesterol. High levels of triglycerides and low levels of HDL cholesterol are both risk factors for cardiovascular disease. High triglycerides have also been associated with insulin resistance and diabetes.

DEBUNKING COMMON MYTHS ABOUT LOW-CARB DIETS

Myths and misinformation about low-carb diets are everywhere. Let's examine a few of these myths and reveal the truth.

Myth 1: low-carb diets increase your risk of heart disease.

This myth is one of the most persistent ones about low-carb diets, but it is based on faulty assumptions, not scientific research.

Because low-carb diets often make up for the reduction in carbs with relatively increased amounts of fat, many in the scientific community have raised the concern that the raised consumption of fat could cause a rise in cholesterol, considered a risk factor for heart disease. Research has shown, however, that people on low-carb, high-fat diets tend to see an improvement in their cholesterol levels. It turns out that when carbohydrates are not available to the body for quick energy, the body is forced to burn fat for energy. So that extra fat, including the saturated fat, is burned before it can hurt you.

Furthermore, recent studies have shown that people on low-carb diets have lower levels of inflammation in their bodies, and inflammation is another risk factor for heart disease.

Although more studies are needed, current research supports the idea that a low-carb, high-fat diet actually protects you from heart disease by improving good cholesterol and reducing triglycerides, insulin resistance, and inflammation.

Myth 2: ketones and ketosis are dangerous side effects of a low-carb diet.

Ketones are substances that are produced naturally in the body during fat metabolism. Ketones are used by various cells, particularly brain cells, for energy and are produced when the supply of dietary carbohydrate is low. People on low-carb diets, then, burn ketones, along with fat, for most of their energy needs. This is called ketosis—when the body burns fat and ketones for energy—and is the goal of many very low-carbohydrate diets.

One concern often raised about ketones and ketosis is that if the body is burning fat for energy, it must not be getting enough glucose, but this is not true. While our bodies can't convert fat to glucose, most cells can use ketones instead of glucose for energy. The body can also make all the glucose it needs by converting glycogen that is stored in the liver tissue and muscles.

Although ketone levels are generally higher in people who eat low-carb diets than in people who eat high-carb diets, restriction of carbohydrates does not typically raise ketones to harmful levels. There is, however, a dangerous condition called ketoacidosis, which is sometimes confused with ketosis. Keto-acidosis is a condition that can develop in sufferers of type 1 diabetes. Because these people are unable to produce insulin, they can accumulate toxic levels of ketones. But this is not a concern for low-carb dieters. Nondiabetics—and even most people with type 2 diabetes who inject insulin—produce enough insulin naturally to prevent ketoacidosis.

Myth 3: counting carbs isn't enough. You have to count calories, too.

For many people, counting carbs is enough because the diet makes them less hungry. While all successful diets may cause weight loss by creating a calorie deficit, low-carb diets create that deficit organically, by altering the body's hormone balance (you'll recall the insulin-leptin-ghrelin cycle) in a way that reduces appetite and increases metabolism. Most people on low-carb diets eat fewer calories but, lucky for them, they don't have to bother counting them since they are simply less hungry.

Myth 4: carbohydrate is an essential nutrient.

An essential nutrient is one that your body needs to survive but cannot create itself. The body has to get essential nutrients from outside sources. There are essential proteins and essential fatty acids, but the body is capable of producing all the carbohydrate it needs for energy.

Myth 5: low-carb diets don't provide all the nutrients you need.

This is another myth that lies very far from the truth. In fact, a low-carb diet based on whole foods (healthy fats, meats, and vegetables) likely provides more fiber, vitamins, and minerals than what has come to be known as the standard American diet, heavy on empty-calorie foods—refined grains and added sugar. The vitamin that is mentioned the most in this debate is vitamin C, but the truth is that meat and green vegetables can provide all of the vitamin C you need.

Myth 6: a low-carb diet causes bone loss and osteoporosis.

This myth is based on the faulty assumption that all low-carb diets are high in protein. In fact, most low-carb diet plans, including the one recommended here, are high in fat with only moderate amounts of protein. Although high-protein diets may cause bone loss, moderate protein is necessary for good bone health and prevention of osteoporosis.

Myth 7: a low-carb diet causes kidney damage.

Again, this myth is based on the faulty assumption that low-carb diets are high in protein. But as mentioned above, low-carb dieters for the most part increase their protein intake by only moderate amounts. So while it is true that eating too much protein can worsen an existing kidney condition, a small increase in protein for low-carb dieters with healthy kidneys does not pose any danger.

CHAPTER 2

Getting Started with the Low-Carb Diet

If you've read this far and have decided that you are ready to lower your carbohydrate intake, there are a few things you should know before you get started.

First and foremost, myths and misinformation about low-carb diets abound. For instance, don't fall for the line that low-carb diets don't allow fruits or vegetables, that it is an inescapably unhealthy way to eat, that it will raise your cholesterol and put you at increased risk for heart disease, or that it has to be difficult and/or boring.

Like other diets, a low-carb diet can be healthy or unhealthy depending on how you go about it. By taking the time to do a bit of research, understanding the difference between good carbs and bad carbs (as well as good fats and bad fats), and devising an eating plan that ensures that you are getting all the nutrients you need, you can lose weight on a low-carb diet while still eating a healthy diet, reducing your risk of disease, and thoroughly enjoying your meals.

HOW MUCH CARBOHYDRATE IS ENOUGH?

There are no hard-and-fast rules about how many grams of carbohydrates you can or should eat. Every body is different. A person's optimal level of carbohydrate intake varies depending on such factors as age, activity level, gender, body composition, and metabolic and overall health. For a healthy, highly active person, an appropriate amount of carb grams per day might be as high as 100, while for a more sedentary person or someone who already produces a lot of insulin, it might be as low as 40 grams (or even lower) per day.

If you are embarking on a low-carb diet to lose weight, your goal is to find a level of carbohydrate intake that makes you feel good and allows you to lose weight without too many negative effects. A good first step for people wishing to lose weight and improve their health through carb reduction is simply to eliminate the very worst carbs from their diets. This includes wheat and wheat products and other highly refined grains (breads, pasta, white rice, many cereals) and foods with added sugar or other caloric sweeteners. By taking this one simple step, you may find that you feel better overall, but it may not be enough to help you lose weight.

If you are serious about losing weight on a low-carb diet, somewhere in the range of 50 to 100 grams of carbohydrates per day is probably where you want to be. Within this range, you can still eat lots of nonstarchy vegetables, some fruits, and very small quantities of starchier vegetables and grains such as potatoes, sweet potatoes, brown rice, or quinoa.

Many low-carb diet plans recommend starting out with an "induction phase" or some other introductory stage, where you restrict carbs even more severely, often as low as 20 to 40 grams per day. This is a great way to achieve what is known as "optimal ketosis," a state in which insulin levels plummet and the body burns fat at a very high rate. Such a low level of carb intake may prove difficult for most people to maintain and could produce negative side effects, such as constipation, dehydration, muscle cramps, and just plain diet burnout. A level somewhere between 50 and 100 grams per day will likely prove more comfortable and more doable for you over a longer time period.

To figure out what level is right for you, track your carb intake when you start out, and simply figure out, through trial and error, what level works best for you. You might want to start with a very low level (50 grams a day, perhaps) and see how you do on that. More than likely, after a bit of an adjustment period, you'll begin to see the weight drop off and find that your appetite is reduced and your cravings all but disappear. On the negative side, you may find that such a low level of carbs leaves you feeling unsatisfied or is simply too much trouble to maintain.

Then, as your body adapts to your new low-carb lifestyle, gradually increase the level of carbohydrates, paying attention to how you feel. If the weight loss slows or stops or if you begin to have strong sugar or carb cravings, reduce your carb level a bit. In this way, you can discover exactly how many carbs you can eat each day while losing weight at the rate you'd like, feeling great, and enjoying life.

ELIMINATE THE BAD CARBS

We have learned that there are two types of carbohydrates: simple (or bad) carbohydrates and complex (or good) carbohydrates. Bad carbohydrates come from highly processed grains and sugars, which are stripped of all their fiber and nutrients; this process leaves only empty calories that cause your blood sugar to spike without any further nutritional benefit. This is okay if you are participating in some physically demanding activity for which you need quick energy. But if you are trying to lose weight, you'll want to steer clear of these bad carbs.

The first step in embarking on a low-carb diet is to make a clean sweep, eliminating all of the bad carbs from your diet and your kitchen: white flour and anything made from white flour (bread, pasta, donuts, etc.), refined sugar and other caloric sweeteners, white potatoes, and white rice.

WHAT ABOUT GOOD CARBS?

Whole grains and foods made from whole grains, vegetables, and fruits contain carbs, too, but these foods are full of fiber and nutrients and are part of a healthful diet, even a low-carb one. The trick is to choose those with the highest nutritional payoff per carbohydrate gram and limit those with very high levels of carbohydrates, such as brown rice or whole-grain pasta, to occasional indulgences.

OKAY, SUGAR'S OUT. WHAT ABOUT ARTIFICIAL SWEETENERS?

Artificial, "non-nutritive" sweeteners differ from caloric sweeteners (sugar, honey, fruit or fruit juice, agave nectar, maple syrup) in that although they taste sweet, they don't contain calories or carbs. As a result, they don't raise blood sugar or insulin levels. This is obviously appealing for anyone who is trying to lose weight, but some research has suggested that, in fact, the use of artificial sweeteners may be associated with increased weight. It might be wiser to simply cut sweets out of your diet than to dabble with these chemical sweeteners that we simply don't know much about. If you do choose to use artificial sweeteners, however, there are many choices available.

Aspartame, sold under the brand names Equal and Nutrasweet, is one of the most common artificial sweeteners. While aspartame is free of carbs and calories, it is not suitable for cooking, cannot be stored for more than a few days, and can cause unpleasant symptoms ranging from mild headaches to serious migraines, stomach upset, and depression.

Sucralose, sold under the brand name Splenda, is synthesized from regular sucrose (sugar) but is composed in a way that renders the molecule unrecognizable to the digestive system so it is not absorbed. It can be used for cooking, although it doesn't taste as good as real sugar. Some sucralose products contain maltodextrin—a carbohydrate made from rice, corn, or potato starch—which is added for bulk. This adds a small amount of carbohydrate and calories, and there is some evidence that it may be harmful to your health. Check the label and use sucralose sparingly.

Sugar alcohols, such as maltitol, xylitol, erythritol, lactitol, and sorbitol, are a class of carbohydrate that is neither sugars nor alcohols. They are widely used as sugar substitutes because they offer the bulk and sweetness of sugar but are not fully absorbed in the digestive system. Hence they are lower in calories and carbs than sugar. As a result, they cause a much slower, smaller blood sugar and insulin spike. Again, these sweeteners should be consumed in limited quantities and with caution since they can cause some nasty side effects, including gas, bloating, and diarrhea.

Stevia is the most natural of the non-nutritive sweeteners since it is an extract derived from a South American plant called stevia (*Stevia rebaudiana*). It is, however, highly processed. Like the artificial sweeteners, it has no carbs or calories. You'll find stevia as a liquid extract or powder in supermarkets and natural food stores. It is heat-stable, so it can be used for cooking and it delivers an intense sweet taste. Use it sparingly, since too much can come across as bitter. Pure stevia is all natural, but many stevia products on the market contain additives such as maltodextrin, dextrose (another natural starch), or the sugar alcohol erythritol, which can cause gas and bloating in some people. Again, check the label and, ideally, use only 100 percent pure stevia extract.

GOOD FATS VERSUS BAD FATS

While low-carb diets are primarily focused on reducing carbohydrates, you do need to pay some attention to the other foods you eat. A low-carb diet does not require you to count or restrict calories, fat grams, cholesterol, or any other nutrient or group of nutrients, but there are a few noncarb foods that should be avoided, as well as some that you should be sure to include as part of a healthy low-carb diet. More specifically, there are good fats that you want to be sure to include in your diet, and there are bad fats that should be avoided.

First, let's talk about good fats, which are an essential part of a healthy low-carb diet. These fats are found naturally in foods, such as meat, dairy products, nuts, legumes, and certain vegetables. The fats found in avocados, eggs, flaxseed, olives and cold-pressed olive oil, coconut and cold-pressed coconut oil, nuts, meat, and fish are all good fats. These fats are made up of a mix of saturated, polyunsaturated, and monounsaturated fats. Omega-3s (found in avocados, fish, olive oil, almonds, and other foods) are among the good fats, but any fat that is found in its natural form in foods and is not heat-processed can be an essential part of a healthy diet.

Good fats help your body absorb nutrients, create hormones, and fight disease. When you are eating a low-carb diet, it is especially important that you include plenty of healthy fats, because these fats are necessary for regulating hormone levels, which contribute to energy levels and weight loss. When you are on a low-carb diet, at least 30 percent to 40 percent of your calories should come from a mix of saturated, polyunsaturated, and monounsaturated fats.

Flaxseed, almonds, salmon, and sardines are all great sources of omega-3s. Eggs and meat contain a beneficial mix of both saturated and unsaturated fat. Coconut and coconut oil contain a particularly good form of fat known as medium chain triglycerides, which may both suppress appetite and boost metabolism. Olives, olive oil, and avocados are rich sources of healthy monounsaturated fat. All of these foods can be incorporated into a healthy, low-carb diet.

Bad fats, on the other hand, should be avoided entirely. Just like bad carbs, bad fats are those that have been processed and damaged. These include highly refined vegetable oils, heat-extracted oils, oils used repeatedly for frying, and hydrogenated or partially hydrogenated oils (trans fats). When highly refined, these oils are stripped of any beneficial nutrients. Furthermore, the body can't break down trans fats, and so they become attached to the arteries, raising your risk for heart disease, stroke, diabetes, and more. These bad fats are found mostly in processed foods like chips, cookies, fast food, prepared food, shortenings, and some margarine.

ALCOHOLIC BEVERAGES

If you're someone who enjoys an alcoholic beverage now and then, you've probably been pleased to read of current research that has found that a bit of alcohol—especially red wine—can be good for your heart. However, you may be wondering how alcoholic beverages fit into a low-carb diet.

Alcoholic beverages are made from high-carb plants, either fruit or grain. During fermentation, much of the carbohydrate is consumed by yeast, which produces alcohol. Alcoholic beverages do contain residual sugar, however, which varies widely by type. A dry wine has very little residual sugar, while a sweet dessert wine has a lot. Distilled spirits, such as vodka or whiskey, have no carbohydrates left after fermentation (but watch out for those high-sugar mixers). Liqueurs have added sugar, so they are the highest in carbohydrates.

The good news is the body treats alcohol differently from carbohydrates, burning those calories before either carbohydrate or fat. On the other hand, alcohol can cause erratic blood pressure. As a result, many popular low-carb diets recommend avoiding alcoholic beverages, either altogether or in the initial phase of the diet. If you do choose to consume alcoholic beverages, choose those that are lower in carbohydrates, such as dry wine or whiskey with non-caloric mixers. Since alcohol can cause blood sugar spikes, it is recommended that alcohol only be consumed with food in order to counteract this effect.

PUTTING IT ALL TOGETHER

By now, you might be feeling overwhelmed with information, but really, low-carb eating is pretty simple. There are just a couple of rules to remember. First, eat meat, fish, eggs, nonroot vegetables (any vegetable that grows above ground), and natural fats such as butter or olive oil. When you do eat carbohydrates, choose whole grains and nonstarchy fruits and vegetables. Second, avoid added sugars, refined grains, and starchy foods like bread, pasta, white rice, and potatoes. Save things like alcohol and chocolate for special treats and consume them in limited quantities. And finally, eat when you feel hungry and stop when you feel satisfied. That's it!

LOW-CARB SHOPPING TIPS

When shopping for food that is consistent with a low-carb diet, start along the outer perimeter of the supermarket. This is where you'll find most of the fresh, whole, natural foods like fresh meat, vegetables, and fruits. Load up your cart with these items and you'll be well on your way to a low-carb meal plan.

When you do venture into the inner aisles of the grocery store, be sure you have your reading glasses handy. Food manufacturers are required to list how many grams of carbohydrates are in each serving on their labels. You'll need to read every label, checking the carbohydrate content as well as the serving size so you know exactly how much carbohydrate you'll be getting for the quantity you are likely to eat in a meal.

The single best piece of low-carb shopping advice is to skip the baked goods aisle altogether. That's right, just don't even go down that aisle if you can avoid it. The same goes for the pasta, cookies, and snack foods aisles.

Three Tips for Low-Carb Shopping Success:
1. Make a list and stick to it.
2. Avoid impulse buys.
3. Never shop on an empty stomach.

STOCKING THE LOW-CARB KITCHEN

Fill your pantry and fridge with delicious whole foods that can be the basis of healthy low-carb meals or quick, grab-and-go low-carb snacks. Load up on nonstarchy fruits and vegetables, fresh fish and shellfish, meats and poultry, dairy products, and nuts and seeds.

Nuts make especially good low-carb snacks because they are loaded with healthy fats, protein, and other nutrients like magnesium, folate, fiber, copper, vitamin E, and arginine. These nutrients all play important roles in the prevention of heart disease. Try sprinkling nuts on salads or yogurt, or just pop them in your mouth instead of carb-heavy chips or crackers.

Choose the right oil. Cold-pressed oil is not damaged in processing the way heat-processed oils are. Cold-pressed olive oil contains healthy, omega-3-rich, monounsaturated fats, and coconut oil also contains medium-chain triglycerides, which suppress appetite and boost metabolism.

TIPS FOR DINING OUT

Dining out can be the most difficult time to stick to any diet regimen. Here are a few ideas to help you get through a restaurant meal with your low-carb status intact.

1. Choose wisely.
If possible, choose a restaurant or style of cuisine that is likely to have low-carb options. For instance, an Italian restaurant or pizzeria would be a hard place to find a low-carb meal. Sauces in Chinese restaurants are often loaded with sugar. Opt for something like Indian or Middle Eastern food that features a lot of vegetables, legumes, and grilled meats.

2. Plan ahead.
If you can't choose the restaurant, try to check the menu ahead of time to see if there are any low-carb options. You might even call the restaurant to ask if it would be possible to substitute cooked vegetables or salad for rice or noodles.

3. Skip white rice and white pasta.
If you can't substitute vegetables, ask if you can substitute brown rice or whole-wheat pasta and then eat only a small amount, or ask for these items to simply be left off your plate.

4. Avoid foods with lots of sauce.
Sauces are delicious, but they often contain loads of hidden sugar and carbohydrates.

5. Be cautious with condiments.
Large doses of carbohydrates hide in condiments such as relish, ketchup, and barbecue sauce, so be sure to check the labels and find alternatives wherever necessary.

COOKING TIPS

Embarking on any new way of eating requires that you learn some new cooking techniques, or perhaps just learn to cook. But cooking healthy, delicious, low-carb meals doesn't have to be difficult. Here are some tips to get you started.

1. **The most important tool: A good chef's knife.**
Low-carb diets often include larger amounts of vegetables than the standard American diet. More vegetables means more chopping. Get yourself a good chef's knife and learn how to use it.

2. **Chop once, eat veggies all week.**
Vegetables are usually quick and easy to cook, but they can be a hassle to prep with all the chopping and slicing that goes into it. Save time by chopping double, triple, or even quadruple what you need for a meal, store them in the fridge, and you'll have quick fixings for the week's meals.

3. **Don't be afraid to substitute frozen vegetables for fresh.**
Frozen vegetables are frozen immediately after harvesting, when they are at their freshest. This means they retain all their nutrients, making them just as nutritious as fresh vegetables, or sometimes even more so. Using frozen vegetables can save on prep time, too, since many come already trimmed and chopped.

4. **Get to know greens.**
Green, leafy vegetables are very low in carbs and full of nutrition—vitamins, minerals, and fiber. There is such a wide variety of greens available that you'll never run out of new ones to try. Delicate greens like lettuce (butter, Bibb, romaine, or red leaf, for instance), baby spinach, arugula, and mâche are all great to eat raw in salads or as wraps for foods that would normally be served inside bread. Sturdier greens like mature spinach, kale, Swiss chard, mustard, and collards are delicious sautéed with smoked or cured meats, garlic, leeks, shallots, or onions.

5. **If you're going to master cooking one thing, make it eggs.**
Eggs are inexpensive, high in protein, quick and easy to cook, and extremely versatile. Learn to make really great eggs and you'll always be just a few minutes away from a fantastic low-carb meal.

6. **Thicken your sauces without adding starch.**
Flour and cornstarch are common sauce thickeners, but there are many ways to thicken a sauce without adding starch. One method is simple reduction—simmering the sauce in an open pan for a long time to let liquid evaporate. Egg yolks are also great thickeners. Vegetable gums are a type of fiber that absorbs liquid, causing sauces to gel. Guar gum and xantham gum are both easy to find at health food stores. Another way to thicken a sauce is simply to add something thick to it, such as sour cream, yogurt, cream cheese, nut butters, or puréed vegetables.

7. Find delicious and nutritious substitutions.

If you miss having a bowl of pasta with sauce, try making zucchini noodles or use spaghetti squash as a pasta substitute. Use large lettuce leaves to wrap burgers or sandwich fillings instead of buns or bread. Purée cauliflower as a delicious substitute for mashed potatoes.

8. Choose your grains wisely.

When you do use grains in your cooking, choose the most nutritious ones. These are whole grains like barley, buckwheat, bulgur, brown rice, corn, millet, and oats. Quinoa is especially popular these days because it is easy to prepare, is delicious hot or cold, and is a complete protein that provides lots of vitamins and minerals, as well as plenty of fiber.

TEN TIPS FOR SUCCESS

When starting a new diet, you likely feel enthusiastic and are full of good intentions and positive thinking. After a few days, however, things might start to get a little rough. To get you started off on the right foot and staying on the path to success, here are ten tips:

1. Do your research.

When starting a low-carb diet, make sure you know what you are getting yourself into. Read up on high- and low-carb foods and think about which foods you will need to eliminate from your meal plan.

2. Get the facts.

Myths about low-carb dieting abound. Read books (this one and many others) and articles to uncover the truth.

3. Be prepared.

Think about situations in which eating low-carb will be a particular challenge and make a plan for how you'll deal with them. If you dine out frequently, do some research to figure out which restaurants and types of cuisine offer the most low-carb choices. If the holidays are coming up, decide how you will resist high-carb foods or perhaps set a limit for yourself to have small amounts as a special treat.

4. Plan your meals.

By planning your meals ahead of time and doing thoughtful grocery shopping, you can ensure that you have the low-carb foods on hand that you enjoy, which will keep you from falling back on old, bad habits.

5. Know the difference between good carbs and bad carbs.

Having a good handle on this information will make it much easier for you to make choices that support a low-carb diet and will help you lose weight. Complex carbohydrates (good carbs) are those found in most vegetables, fruits, and whole grains. The closer a food is to its natural form, the higher quality of carbohydrates it contains. Simple carbohydrates (bad carbs) are those found in high-calorie foods that offer little fiber and few nutrients, like refined grains (white flour, white rice, etc.), added sugars, and starchy vegetables like white potatoes.

6. Eat your veggies (and fruit, too)!

There is a common misperception that vegetables and fruit are not compatible with a low-carb diet since they contain carbohydrates. This is simply not true. Remember the earlier discussion of good carbs versus bad carbs? Most vegetables and many fruits fall into the good-carbs category and they are essential for good health. Vegetables and fruits contain fiber and micronutrients that will keep you feeling satisfied and give you energy throughout the day.

7. Eat plenty of fiber.

Reducing grains in your diet has one unfortunate effect, which is that it cuts out a big source of fiber. Although fiber is a carbohydrate, it is not digested the way other carbs are, so it acts completely differently in your body. In fact, fiber is extremely important for digestive health. There are many low-carb, high-fiber foods, including many vegetables, that can provide the fiber you need.

8. Don't be afraid of dietary fat.

Remember, good fat (the type found naturally in foods, such as meat, dairy products, nuts, legumes, and certain vegetables) is an essential part of a healthy diet. Good fats help your body absorb nutrients, create hormones, and fight disease. These fats are necessary for regulating hormone levels, which contribute to energy levels and weight loss. When you are on a low-carb diet, at least 30 percent to 40 percent of your calories should come from a mix of saturated, polyunsaturated, and monounsaturated fats.

9. Drink plenty of water.

This admonition comes along with any diet plan, but that's because it is important for good health and because it works. Initial weight loss on any diet is usually the result of water loss, so drink lots of water to keep you from becoming dehydrated. Dehydration slows down the fat-burning process, which is not what you want. It can also sap your energy and make you constipated, especially if you are eating lots of fiber. And water fills you up so that you need to eat less food in order to feel satisfied.

10. Get your exercise.

Exercise can speed up your weight loss, but it's also important for cardiovascular and respiratory health. Plus, it just makes you feel good.

CHAPTER 3

The Meal Plan

Starting any new lifestyle habit—whether it is an exercise plan or a diet—is challenging, since habits are deeply ingrained and often hard to break or even bend. Having a detailed plan is a great way to get you started on the right track. It's like a road map that shows you exactly where to turn each step of the way.

This seven-day meal plan is designed to help you start the first week of the low-carb diet with ease. It is designed for an average adult with a limit of 50 to 75 grams of carbs per day. Feel free to make adjustments, depending on personal factors such as your weight, age, activity level, and carbohydrate sensitivity. For instance, if you are very active, you may wish to add more carbs—perhaps a total of 100 grams or more per day might be suitable.

Remember that your low-carb diet is a lifestyle change, not a quick fix. You might find that after just a few weeks on the diet, your weight will drop, you'll have more energy, and, perhaps the best part, you won't feel nearly as hungry. But don't fall into the trap of thinking that you've fixed the problem and can go back to your old habits. Returning to a high-carb diet will only ensure weight gain will come back to haunt you again.

The good news is that once you've been on the diet for a few weeks, you'll find that choosing low-carb foods becomes second nature. You won't have to think so much about every morsel of food you put in your mouth. Soon you will be eating a low-carb diet as a matter of course—and you'll be less hungry and have more energy.

The meal plan includes many of the recipes from Part Two of this book. These recipes are all easy to make, full of flavor, and low in carbs.

HOW TO USE THIS LOW-CARB DIET MEAL PLAN

This meal plan is not meant to be a rigid rule book, but rather a guideline to help you get a sense of what you can eat in a day and still keep your carb intake low. If there are any dishes on the plan that you don't care for, simply switch them out for something else.

This meal plan is designed for a moderately active person who is trying to lose weight, so each day's plan adds up to no more than 75 grams of carbohydrates. If you are extremely active or need a much higher calorie diet than most, you may need to add foods or increase portions to reach your calorie and carbohydrate needs.

On the other hand, if you are having trouble losing weight even while eating only 50 grams of carbs per day, or if you find you still crave high-carb foods, try reducing your portion size or eliminating foods with even moderate carbohydrate levels to get under 50 grams of carbohydrates per day.

SEVEN-DAY MEAL PLAN

Day One (61.2 grams carbs)

Breakfast: Spring Pea and Mint Frittata with Goat Cheese and Pancetta (17.1 grams carbs)
Lunch: Butternut Squash and Chipotle Soup (18.3 grams carbs)
Snack/Appetizer: Cabbage-Wrapped Fresh Thai Spring Rolls (9.7 grams carbs)
Dinner: Roasted Salmon with Caramelized Leeks (6.4 grams carbs)
Dessert: Chocolate and Vanilla Meringue Swirls (9.7 grams carbs)

Day Two (53 grams carbs)

Breakfast: Glazed Cinnamon Roll Muffins (15.1 grams carbs)
Lunch: Kale and Almond Salad with Parmesan Cheese and Lemon Vinaigrette (14 grams carbs)
Snack/Appetizer: Baked Barbecued Zucchini Chips (9.5 grams carbs)
Dinner: Seared Trout with Cherry Tomatoes and Bacon (4.7 grams carbs)
Dessert: Chocolate and Vanilla Meringue Swirls (9.7 grams carbs)

Day Three (63.8 grams carbs)

Breakfast: Bacon-Crusted Mini Quiches with Mushrooms and Greens (3.9 grams carbs)
Lunch: Creamy Chicken Soup with Roasted Garlic (9.9 grams carbs)
Snack/Appetizer: Orange Cream Ice Pops (11.8 grams carbs)
Dinner: Quinoa and Vegetable Gratin (29.7 grams carbs)
Dessert: Frosted Brownies (8.5 grams carbs)

Day Four (60.4 grams carbs)

Breakfast: No-Bake Peanut Butter–Coconut Protein Bars (21.8 grams carbs)
Lunch: Roasted Cauliflower Soup with Smoked Gouda (12.3 grams carbs)
Snack/Appetizer: Olive Tapenade–Filled Cucumber Bites (5.8 grams carbs)
Dinner: Garlic-Lime Shrimp and Peppers (9 grams carbs)
Dessert: Chocolate-Filled Strawberry Soufflés (11.5 grams carbs)

Day Five (63.5 grams carbs)

Breakfast: Savory Cottage Cheese Muffins (6.4 grams carbs)
Lunch: Radicchio, Fennel, and Orange Salad with Olive Vinaigrette
(20.5 grams carbs)
Snack/Appetizer: Cherries and Chocolate Snack Bars (17 grams carbs)
Dinner: Seared Chicken Veracruz (10.2 grams carbs)
Dessert: Cinnamon-Pecan Thins (9.4 grams carbs)

Day Six (50 grams carbs)

Breakfast: Prosciutto, Spinach, and Cream Baked Eggs (7.8 grams carbs)
Lunch: Steak Salad with Blue Cheese Dressing (3.6 grams carbs)
Snack/Appetizer: Crispy Parmesan Kale Chips (17.5 grams carbs)
Dinner: Prosciutto-Wrapped Chicken Stuffed with Goat Cheese
(0.8 grams carbs)
Dessert: Carrot Cake with Whipped Coconut Cream Frosting
(20.3 grams carbs)

Day Seven (53.4 grams carbs)

Breakfast: Fluffy Almond Pancakes with Fresh Berries (13.6 grams carbs)
Lunch: Cobb Salad (9 grams carbs)
Snack/Appetizer: Bacon-Chile-Cheese Bites with Pecans (3.1 grams carbs)
Dinner: Pizza Margherita with a Cauliflower Crust (16.9 grams carbs)
Dessert: Nut-Crusted Mini Maple Cheesecakes (10.8 grams carbs)

PART TWO

Recipes

CHAPTER FOUR BREAKFAST

CHAPTER FIVE APPETIZERS AND SNACKS

CHAPTER SIX SOUPS AND SALADS

CHAPTER SEVEN ENTRÉES

CHAPTER EIGHT DESSERTS

CHAPTER 4

Breakfast

SPRING PEA AND MINT FRITTATA WITH GOAT CHEESE AND PANCETTA

PROSCIUTTO, SPINACH, AND CREAM BAKED EGGS

BACON-CRUSTED MINI QUICHES WITH MUSHROOMS AND GREENS

CRISPY CAULIFLOWER PANCAKES

SAVORY COTTAGE CHEESE MUFFINS

FLUFFY ALMOND PANCAKES WITH FRESH BERRIES

NO-BAKE PEANUT BUTTER—COCONUT PROTEIN BARS

GLAZED CINNAMON ROLL MUFFINS

Spring Pea and Mint Frittata with Goat Cheese and Pancetta

SERVES 6

PER SERVING:

- ▶ CALORIES: 334
- ▶ FAT (GRAMS): 19.3
- ▶ CHOLESTEROL (MILLIGRAMS): 279
- ▶ SODIUM (MILLIGRAMS): 712
- ▶ CARBOHYDRATES (GRAMS): 17.1
- ▶ FIBER (GRAMS): 5.5
- ▶ PROTEIN (GRAMS): 23.4

This pretty frittata is quick to make and can be served hot, warm, or at room temperature. It's a great make-ahead weekday breakfast or festive brunch. Wrap the leftovers in plastic wrap and store in the refrigerator. Reheat in the microwave. Feel free to substitute thick-cut bacon for the pancetta.

2 TEASPOONS OLIVE OIL

1 SMALL SHALLOT, DICED

1 GARLIC CLOVE, MINCED

2 OUNCES PANCETTA, DICED

4 CUPS ARUGULA

2 CUPS FROZEN PEAS, THAWED

8 EGGS

2 TABLESPOONS MILK

¾ TEASPOON SALT

4 OUNCES CRUMBLED GOAT CHEESE

2 TABLESPOONS CHOPPED FRESH MINT

1. Preheat the oven to 450°F.

2. In a large, oven-safe, nonstick skillet over medium-high heat, heat the oil. Add the shallot, garlic, and pancetta and cook, stirring frequently, until the

shallot is soft, about 5 minutes. Add the arugula and peas and cook just until the arugula is wilted, 1 to 2 minutes.

3. Meanwhile, in a medium bowl, whisk together the eggs, milk, and salt. Add half of the goat cheese to the eggs along with the mint. Whisk to combine.

4. Pour the egg mixture over the vegetables in the skillet. Transfer the skillet to the preheated oven and cook until the top is almost set, about 8 to 10 minutes. Remove from the oven and turn on the broiler.

5. Crumble the remaining goat cheese over the top of the frittata and place the skillet under the broiler. Broil for 2 to 3 minutes, until the cheese is golden brown and bubbling.

6. Let the frittata sit in the pan for a few minutes, then turn it out on a plate and cut it into six wedges. Serve hot, or wrap cooled portions and refrigerate or freeze.

Prosciutto, Spinach, and Cream Baked Eggs

SERVES 4

PER SERVING:

- ▶ CALORIES: 303
- ▶ FAT (GRAMS): 24.3
- ▶ CHOLESTEROL (MILLIGRAMS): 251
- ▶ SODIUM (MILLIGRAMS): 819
- ▶ CARBOHYDRATES (GRAMS): 7.8
- ▶ FIBER (GRAMS): 3.8
- ▶ PROTEIN (GRAMS): 16.8

These baked eggs are easy to make, but the addition of prosciutto and heavy cream make them luxurious. This dish is perfect for a weekend brunch, or even for a light dinner.

2 TABLESPOONS UNSALTED BUTTER

1½ POUNDS SPINACH, TRIMMED AND RINSED

1 TEASPOON OLIVE OIL

3 OUNCES PROSCIUTTO, CHOPPED

¾ CUP HEAVY CREAM, PLUS 4 TEASPOONS

½ TEASPOON SALT

¼ TEASPOON PEPPER

A FEW GRATINGS OF FRESH NUTMEG

4 EGGS

2 TABLESPOONS GRATED PARMESAN CHEESE

1. Preheat the oven to 350°F.

2. Melt 1 tablespoon of the butter in a 6-ounce ramekin in the microwave and use the melted butter to coat the inside of the ramekin and three other 6-ounce ramekins. Arrange the ramekins on a baking sheet.

3. In a large saucepan over medium heat, add the remaining 1 tablespoon of the butter and melt it. Add the spinach, a few handfuls at a time, and cook, turning, until it wilts before adding more. Drain the spinach and squeeze out any excess water. Chop the spinach.

4. Wipe out the saucepan, add the olive oil, and heat over medium heat. Cook the prosciutto, stirring for about 2 minutes, until the fat begins to render. Stir in the spinach and ¾ cup of the cream and cook, stirring frequently, until the mixture comes to a boil and the cream becomes very thick and is reduced to about ¼ cup, 3 to 5 minutes. Stir in the salt, pepper, and nutmeg.

5. Divide the sauce among the four prepared ramekins. Crack an egg into a small bowl and check for bits of shell, then pour the egg into each ramekin, season each with salt and pepper, and drizzle 1 teaspoon of the remaining cream over each.

6. Bake until the whites of the egg are set and just beginning to brown around the edges. Sprinkle the Parmesan cheese over the eggs and serve immediately.

Bacon-Crusted Mini Quiches with Mushrooms and Greens

MAKES 8 MINI QUICHES

PER SERVING:

- CALORIES: 182
- FAT (GRAMS): 13.1
- CHOLESTEROL
(MILLIGRAMS): 144

- SODIUM (MILLIGRAMS): 824
- CARBOHYDRATES (GRAMS): 3.9
- FIBER (GRAMS): 1.2
- PROTEIN (GRAMS): 12.7

These delicious, portable breakfast quiches make a terrific on-the-go breakfast. They can be prepared in advance and stored in the fridge or freezer, and then heated in the microwave just before you dash out the door.

8 STRIPS BACON

1 TABLESPOON OLIVE OIL

1 SMALL ONION, CHOPPED

3 TO 4 BUTTON OR CREMINI MUSHROOMS, CHOPPED

1 POUND SWISS CHARD, STEMMED AND CUT INTO RIBBONS

6 EGGS

¾ TEASPOON SALT

¼ TEASPOON PEPPER

1. Preheat the oven to 350°F. In a standard muffin tin, place a strip of bacon into each of eight cups, wrapping the bacon around the edge to form a bottomless cup.

2. Heat the olive oil in a medium skillet over medium-high heat. Add the onion and mushrooms and cook, stirring, until they begin to soften, about 3 minutes. Add the chard and cook until wilted, 3 to 4 minutes more.

3. In a medium bowl, whisk the eggs with the salt and pepper until well beaten. Stir the vegetable mixture into the eggs, then ladle the egg mixture into the eight bacon-lined muffin cups, dividing it equally.

4. Bake until puffed and golden, about 30 minutes. Serve immediately, or cool to room temperature and store in the fridge for up to 5 days or in the freezer for up to 3 months.

Crispy Cauliflower Pancakes

SERVES 4

PER SERVING:

- ▶ CALORIES: 372
- ▶ FAT (GRAMS): 27.1
- ▶ CHOLESTEROL (MILLIGRAMS): 186
- ▶ SODIUM (MILLIGRAMS): 729
- ▶ CARBOHYDRATES (GRAMS): 15.4
- ▶ FIBER (GRAMS): 14.2
- ▶ PROTEIN (GRAMS): 6.1

These veggie-filled pancakes are somewhat like fritters and make for a super-easy and healthy meal. They are low in carbs, but yummy. Plus, they are full of protein and fiber, so they'll keep you feeling full all morning long. The pancakes reheat nicely in the microwave, so make extra and stash a few in the fridge for another day.

1 LARGE HEAD CAULIFLOWER, CUT INTO SMALL FLORETS

2 MEDIUM CARROTS, GRATED

4 EGGS

½ CUP FLAXSEED MEAL

½ CUP RAW UNSALTED SUNFLOWER SEEDS

½ CUP FINELY CHOPPED HAZELNUTS

½ CUP FINELY CHOPPED FRESH PARSLEY

2 TEASPOONS FRESH LIME JUICE

1 TEASPOON SALT

½ TEASPOON BLACK PEPPER

2 TEASPOONS FRESH THYME

1 TEASPOON SMOKED PAPRIKA

½ TEASPOON CAYENNE PEPPER

2 TABLESPOONS OLIVE OIL, PLUS MORE IF NEEDED

1. Place the cauliflower in a food processor and pulse until it resembles coarse meal. Transfer to a large mixing bowl.

2. Add the carrots, eggs, flaxseed meal, sunflower seeds, hazelnuts, parsley, lime juice, salt, black pepper, thyme, paprika, and cayenne pepper. Stir to combine well.

3. Heat the olive oil in a medium nonstick skillet over medium-high heat. Spoon the batter into the pan about ¼ cup at a time. Smooth each flat with the back of measuring cup or ladle.

4. Cook until the pancakes are golden brown, about 3 minutes per side. Repeat until you have used up all the batter, adding a bit more oil to the skillet if needed.

5. Serve immediately.

Savory Cottage Cheese Muffins

MAKES 9 MUFFINS

PER SERVING:

- CALORIES: 126
- FAT (GRAMS): 7.2
- CHOLESTEROL
(MILLIGRAMS): 89

- SODIUM (MILLIGRAMS): 353
- CARBOHYDRATES (GRAMS): 6.4
- FIBER (GRAMS): 1.3
- PROTEIN (GRAMS): 9.9

These savory muffins are loaded with protein. Studded with sun-dried tomatoes, olives, and fresh oregano, they are also full of flavor.

1 CUP LOW-FAT COTTAGE CHEESE

¾ CUP GRATED PARMESAN CHEESE

¼ CUP WHITE WHOLE-WHEAT FLOUR

½ CUP ALMOND MEAL

1 TEASPOON BAKING POWDER

¼ CUP SUN-DRIED TOMATOES IN OIL, DRAINED AND FINELY CHOPPED

¼ CUP CHOPPED KALAMATA OLIVES

2 TABLESPOONS FINELY CHOPPED FRESH OREGANO

¼ CUP WATER

4 EGGS, LIGHTLY BEATEN

½ TEASPOON SALT

1. Preheat the oven to 400°F. Line the cups of a standard muffin tin with nine paper liners.

2. In a large bowl, combine cottage cheese, ½ cup Parmesan cheese, flour, almond meal, baking powder, sun-dried tomatoes, olives, oregano, water, eggs, and salt. Mix well.

3. Spoon the mixture into the prepared muffin cups, dividing equally. The cups should be about three-fourths full. Sprinkle the remaining Parmesan cheese over the tops.

4. Bake until the muffins are puffy and golden brown, 30 to 35 minutes. Serve warm or at room temperature.

Fluffy Almond Pancakes with Fresh Berries

SERVES 6

PER SERVING:

▶ CALORIES: 322

▶ FAT (GRAMS): 24.4

▶ CHOLESTEROL (MILLIGRAMS): 124

▶ SODIUM (MILLIGRAMS): 74

▶ CARBOHYDRATES (GRAMS): 13.6

▶ FIBER (GRAMS): 5.7

▶ PROTEIN (GRAMS): 4.5

These simple, fluffy pancakes are every bit as delicious as their carb-heavy kin. They are easily adapted to be sweet or savory. For instance, try adding ricotta cheese, lemon zest, vanilla extract, or cinnamon for sweet versions. Or add sour cream, chopped chives, fresh oregano or basil, chopped nuts, or crumbled bacon for savory versions.

2 CUPS ALMOND MEAL

4 EGGS, LIGHTLY BEATEN

½ CUP WATER

1 TEASPOON CANOLA OR OLIVE OIL

1 TEASPOON HONEY OR AGAVE NECTAR

PINCH OF SALT

COOKING SPRAY

2 CUPS FRESH BERRIES (RASPBERRIES, STRAWBERRIES, BLACKBERRIES, BLUEBERRIES, OR A COMBINATION)

1. In a large bowl, combine the almond meal, eggs, water, oil, honey, and salt and stir until well combined and smooth.

2. Heat a large nonstick skillet coated with cooking spray over medium-high heat.

3. Ladle the batter into the pan, about ¼ cup at a time. Cook until bubbles start to appear on the top, about 2 minutes, then flip the pancakes over and cook until golden on the second side, about 2 minutes more. Repeat until all of the batter has been cooked, adding cooking spray to the skillet between batches as needed.

4. Serve immediately topped with the berries.

No-Bake Peanut Butter–Coconut Protein Bars

MAKES 12 BARS

PER SERVING:

- ▶ CALORIES: 209
- ▶ FAT (GRAMS): 8
- ▶ CHOLESTEROL (MILLIGRAMS): 17
- ▶ SODIUM (MILLIGRAMS): 129
- ▶ CARBOHYDRATES (GRAMS): 21.8
- ▶ FIBER (GRAMS): 2.3
- ▶ PROTEIN (GRAMS): 11.1

These tasty bars are full of protein and take only minutes to make. You can substitute any nut butter you like and use a noncaloric sweetener (like sucralose) if you prefer. Keep a bag of these treats in the freezer and you'll always have a healthy breakfast or snack on hand.

1½ CUPS OLD-FASHIONED ROLLED OATS, PROCESSED TO A FLOUR

½ CUP UNSWEETENED PROTEIN POWDER

½ CUP CRISP RICE CEREAL

¼ TEASPOON SALT

½ CUP NO-SUGAR-ADDED, ALL-NATURAL PEANUT BUTTER

½ CUP PURE MAPLE SYRUP, AGAVE NECTAR, OR OTHER LIQUID SWEETENER

1 TEASPOON VANILLA EXTRACT

3 TABLESPOONS SUGAR-FREE SEMISWEET CHOCOLATE CHIPS

½ TABLESPOON COCONUT OIL

1. Line an 8-inch square pan with parchment paper.

2. In a large bowl, combine the oat flour, protein powder, rice cereal, and salt. Add the peanut butter, maple syrup, and vanilla and stir to mix well.

3. Press the mixture into the prepared pan, smoothing the top evenly.

4. Chill pan in the freezer for about 15 minutes.

5. Meanwhile, in a small glass bowl, melt the chocolate chips and coconut oil together in the microwave at 50 percent power for 30-second intervals. When the chips begin to melt, stir with a fork until smooth.

6. Remove the pan from the freezer and slice into twelve bars. Set the bars on a platter or baking sheet with a bit of space between them and drizzle the melted chocolate over the tops. Freeze again until the chocolate is set, about 15 minutes more. Serve immediately or transfer the bars to a sealable, freezer-safe plastic bag and store for up to 3 months.

Glazed Cinnamon Roll Muffins

MAKES 8 MUFFINS

PER SERVING:

- ▶ CALORIES: 231
- ▶ FAT (GRAMS): 13.8
- ▶ CHOLESTEROL (MILLIGRAMS): 93
- ▶ SODIUM (MILLIGRAMS): 166
- ▶ CARBOHYDRATES (GRAMS): 15.1
- ▶ FIBER (GRAMS): 5.3
- ▶ PROTEIN (GRAMS): 6.2

These low-carb muffins really capture the flavor of forbidden cinnamon buns. Serve them warm or at room temperature for a special treat that's healthful enough to eat any day of the week.

MUFFINS:

½ CUP FLAXSEED MEAL

¼ CUP COCONUT FLOUR

¼ CUP SUCRALOSE OR OTHER NONCALORIC GRANULATED SWEETENER

1 TEASPOON BAKING POWDER

1 TEASPOON GROUND CINNAMON

¼ TEASPOON SALT

3 EGGS

¼ CUP UNSWEETENED ALMOND MILK, PLUS MORE IF NEEDED

2 TABLESPOONS UNSALTED BUTTER, MELTED AND COOLED

1 TEASPOON VANILLA EXTRACT

TOPPING:

¼ CUP SUCRALOSE OR OTHER NONCALORIC GRANULATED SWEETENER

2 TABLESPOONS UNSALTED BUTTER, MELTED

1 TEASPOON GROUND CINNAMON

2 TABLESPOONS PECANS

GLAZE:

1 TABLESPOON UNSALTED BUTTER, AT ROOM TEMPERATURE

1 TABLESPOON CREAM CHEESE, AT ROOM TEMPERATURE

1 TABLESPOON HEAVY CREAM

¼ TEASPOON LIQUID NONCALORIC SWEETENER, SUCH AS STEVIA

Preheat the oven to 325°F. Line a standard muffin tin with paper liners.

For the Muffins:

1. In a medium bowl, add the flaxseed meal, coconut flour, sweetener, baking powder, cinnamon, and salt and stir to combine.

2. In a small bowl, whisk the eggs until lightly beaten. Add the almond milk, butter, and vanilla and whisk to combine.

3. Add the egg mixture to the flaxseed mixture and stir to combine. If the batter is too thick, add a bit more almond milk.

For the Topping:

1. In a small bowl, combine the sweetener, butter, cinnamon, and pecans.

2. Spoon the batter into the prepared muffin tin. Each muffin cup should be about three-fourths full. Sprinkle the topping equally over the muffins, about 1 teaspoon each.

3. Bake until the tops are lightly browned and a toothpick inserted into the center comes out clean, 35 to 40 minutes. Let the muffins cool in the pan for a few minutes, then turn out onto a rack.

For the Glaze:

Stir together the butter and cream cheese. Add the cream and liquid sweetener and stir until smooth. Drizzle the glaze over the tops of the warm muffins and serve immediately. The muffins can be frozen and stored for up to 3 months.

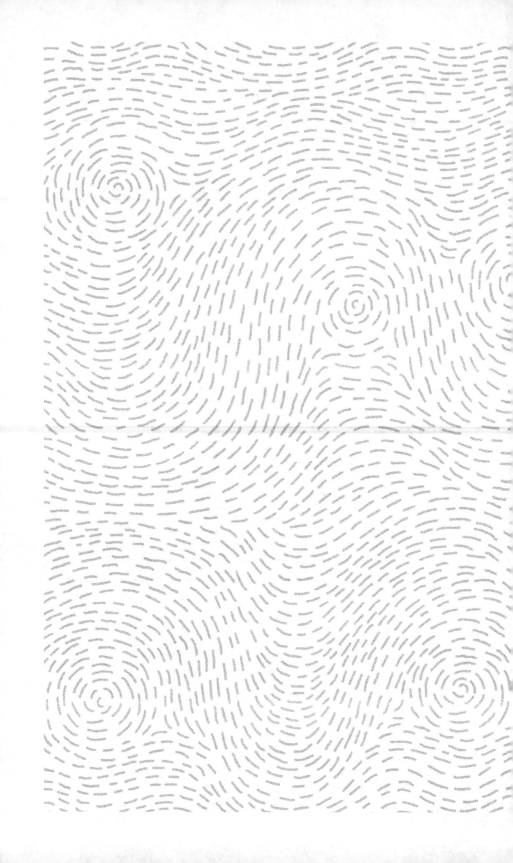

CHAPTER 5

Appetizers and Snacks

CRISPY PARMESAN KALE CHIPS

BAKED BARBECUE ZUCCHINI CHIPS

BACON-CHILE-CHEESE BITES WITH PECANS

OLIVE TAPENADE—FILLED CUCUMBER BITES

CABBAGE-WRAPPED FRESH THAI SPRING ROLLS

ORANGE CREAM ICE POPS

CHOCOLATE SHAKE

CHERRY AND CHOCOLATE SNACK BARS

Crispy Parmesan Kale Chips

SERVES 4

PER SERVING:

▶ CALORIES: 251

▶ FAT (GRAMS): 18.6

▶ CHOLESTEROL
(MILLIGRAMS): 10

▶ SODIUM (MILLIGRAMS): 786

▶ CARBOHYDRATES
(GRAMS): 17.5

▶ FIBER (GRAMS): 3.4

▶ PROTEIN (GRAMS): 10.2

These crispy, salty, cheesy chips are a fantastic healthy alternative to potato chips or to any salty snack you might be craving. Kale is one of the most nutrient-dense foods on the planet. Crunchy and flavorful, these chips will help you meet your daily requirement of vegetables.

1 BUNCH CURLY LEAF KALE

2 TABLESPOONS OLIVE OIL

¼ CUP (ABOUT 1 OUNCE) GRATED PARMESAN CHEESE

½ TEASPOON SALT

1. Preheat the oven to 375°F.

2. Make sure the kale is very dry. Tear the kale into bite-size pieces.

3. In a large bowl, toss the kale with the olive oil. Lay it in a single layer on a large baking sheet, and sprinkle with a pinch or two of salt.

4. Bake until the kale is crispy, 10 to 15 minutes. Sprinkle the Parmesan over the top and bake for another 5 minutes. Serve immediately or store the chips in an airtight container at room temperature for up to 3 days.

Baked Barbecue Zucchini Chips

SERVES 2

PER SERVING:

- ▶ CALORIES: 46
- ▶ FAT (GRAMS): 0.8
- ▶ CHOLESTEROL (MILLIGRAMS): 0
- ▶ SODIUM (MILLIGRAMS): 895
- ▶ CARBOHYDRATES (GRAMS): 9.5
- ▶ FIBER (GRAMS): 2.8
- ▶ PROTEIN (GRAMS): 2.9

A mandoline makes quick work of slicing the zucchini and enables you to get very thin rounds. But if you don't have one, a sharp knife and a bit of patience will work just as well. Try using one green zucchini and one yellow zucchini for visual effect, or get creative and use other vegetables like butternut squash, eggplant, parsnips, or carrots.

SEASONING MIX:

1 TEASPOON PAPRIKA

1 TEASPOON GROUND CUMIN

½ TEASPOON CHILI POWDER

½ TEASPOON ONION POWDER

½ TEASPOON GARLIC POWDER

¼ TEASPOON PEPPER

½ TEASPOON LIGHT BROWN SUGAR

¾ TEASPOON SALT

CHIPS:

2 MEDIUM ZUCCHINI, SLICED INTO VERY THIN ROUNDS

CANOLA OIL COOKING SPRAY

continued ▶

Preheat oven to 375°F. Coat a large rimmed baking sheet with cooking spray.

For the Seasoning Mix:

In a small bowl, combine spices with sugar and salt until well mixed.

For the Chips:

1. Arrange the zucchini slices in a single layer on the prepared baking sheet (you may need to use two sheets) and coat the slices lightly with more cooking spray. Sprinkle with some of the seasoning mixture (you can add more later).

2. Bake for 30 to 40 minutes. Rotate the pan or, if using two pans, switch them around and continue to bake until the chips are browned and crisp, another 30 to 45 minutes.

3. Remove from the oven and let cool for a couple of minutes, then transfer to a bowl and serve, sprinkling with additional seasoning if desired.

Bacon-Chile-Cheese Bites with Pecans

MAKES 16 BITES

PER SERVING:

- ▶ CALORIES: 350
- ▶ FAT (GRAMS): 32.7
- ▶ CHOLESTEROL
(MILLIGRAMS): 84

- ▶ SODIUM (MILLIGRAMS): 535
- ▶ CARBOHYDRATES (GRAMS): 3.1
- ▶ FIBER (GRAMS): 0.8
- ▶ PROTEIN (GRAMS): 12

Pecans are full of healthy fats that protect you against cardiovascular and other diseases by lowering your cholesterol. The welcome nutty crunch pairs well with the creamy cheese and smoky bacon. These scrumptious bites will satisfy big appetites.

16 OUNCES CREAM CHEESE, AT ROOM TEMPERATURE

½ CUP FIRE-ROASTED DICED TOMATOES WITH GREEN CHILES

½ CUP CHOPPED PECANS

6 STRIPS BACON, COOKED AND CRUMBLED

½ CUP SHREDDED MONTEREY JACK CHEESE

1. In a medium bowl, combine the cream cheese and tomatoes until well-mixed. Chill mixture in the refrigerator for 30 minutes.

2. Shape the cream cheese mixture into 16 balls, about 1 inch in diameter.

3. In a small shallow bowl, combine the pecans, bacon, and shredded Jack cheese. Roll each cream cheese ball in the pecan-bacon mixture to coat the outside and place on a baking sheet.

4. When all the balls are coated, put the baking sheet in the refrigerator and chill until firm, about 30 minutes. Transfer to a platter and serve.

Olive Tapenade–Filled Cucumber Bites

SERVES 4

PER SERVING:

- CALORIES: 59
- FAT (GRAMS): 4.4
- CHOLESTEROL (MILLIGRAMS): 0
- SODIUM (MILLIGRAMS): 276
- CARBOHYDRATES (GRAMS): 5.8
- FIBER (GRAMS): 1.8
- PROTEIN (GRAMS): 1

These elegant-looking bites stand in for carb-heavy canapés. They are crunchy, salty, and full of flavor but low in carbs. Enjoy them while watching the game on TV or serve them as a passed appetizer at your next cocktail party.

1 ENGLISH CUCUMBER

2 TABLESPOONS CAPERS, DRAINED, RINSED, AND MINCED

½ CUP PITTED KALAMATA OLIVES, RINSED AND MINCED

1 TABLESPOON FINELY DICED RED ONION

1 TABLESPOON FINELY DICED RED BELL PEPPER

1 GARLIC CLOVE, MINCED

1 TABLESPOON FRESH LEMON ZEST

1 TABLESPOON FINELY CHOPPED FRESH OREGANO

¼ TEASPOON CRUSHED RED PEPPER FLAKES

2 TEASPOONS OLIVE OIL

1. Slice the cucumber into rounds about ½-inch thick. Using a small teaspoon, scoop some of the seeds from each cucumber round to make a bowl, leaving the bottom layer of seeds intact.

2. In a small bowl, combine the capers, olives, onion, bell pepper, garlic, lemon zest, oregano, red pepper flakes, and olive oil and stir to combine.

3. Spoon the tapenade into each cucumber "bowl," using about a heaped tablespoon of filling for each. Serve immediately.

Cabbage-Wrapped Fresh Thai Spring Rolls

MAKES 4 ROLLS

PER SERVING:

▶ CALORIES: 79

▶ FAT (GRAMS): 0.7

▶ CHOLESTEROL (MILLIGRAMS): 60

▶ SODIUM (MILLIGRAMS): 210

▶ CARBOHYDRATES (GRAMS): 9.7

▶ FIBER (GRAMS): 1.4

▶ PROTEIN (GRAMS): 7.4

This easy appetizer delivers the bright flavors of Thai spring rolls in a low-carb cabbage leaf. The dipping sauce is a departure from the usual sugar-laden peanut sauce, but rest assured, it is full of delicious flavor.

ROLLS:

4 LARGE CABBAGE LEAVES

8 MEDIUM UNCOOKED SHRIMP, PEELED, DEVEINED, AND HALVED LENGTHWISE (ABOUT 4 OUNCES)

½ MEDIUM CUCUMBER, PEELED, SEEDED, AND JULIENNED

1 MEDIUM CARROT, JULIENNED

4 GREEN ONIONS, JULIENNED

8 FRESH BASIL LEAVES

12 FRESH MINT LEAVES

DIPPING SAUCE:

3 TABLESPOONS RICE VINEGAR

1 TABLESPOON HONEY

1 TEASPOON FISH SAUCE*

⅛ TEASPOON THAI RED CURRY PASTE

continued ▶

For the Rolls:

1. Bring a large pot of water to a boil. Add the cabbage leaves and cook until softened, 2 to 3 minutes. Drain and transfer to a bowl of ice water to stop the cooking.

2. Bring a medium saucepan of lightly salted water to a boil. Add the shrimp, reduce the heat to medium-low, and simmer until the shrimp are pink and cooked through, about 2 to 3 minutes. Drain and place the shrimp in a bowl of ice water to stop the cooking.

3. To make the rolls, on one cabbage leaf, lay 2 of the shrimp in a row along the top, rounded part of one of the cabbage leaves. Add one-fourth of the cucumbers, carrot, green onions, basil, and mint. Roll up from the rounded part of the leaf toward the root end. Place on a plate seam-side down. Repeat with the remaining leaves and filling.

For the Dipping Sauce:

1. In a small bowl, combine the rice vinegar, honey, fish sauce, and curry paste, and whisk until smooth.

2. Serve the cabbage rolls immediately with the dipping sauce, or tightly wrap the rolls in plastic wrap and refrigerate for up to 2 days. The sauce can be stored in a covered container in the refrigerator for up to a week.

*Note that fish sauce often contains crab and other shellfish. If you or a loved one are sensitive to shellfish, substitute soy sauce or miso paste.

Orange Cream Ice Pops

MAKES 10 ICE POPS

PER SERVING:

- ▶ CALORIES: 58
- ▶ FAT (GRAMS): 0.4
- ▶ CHOLESTEROL (MILLIGRAMS): 3
- ▶ SODIUM (MILLIGRAMS): 26
- ▶ CARBOHYDRATES (GRAMS): 11.8
- ▶ FIBER (GRAMS): 0
- ▶ PROTEIN (GRAMS): 1.9

These refreshing ice pops will transport you back to the lazy days of childhood summers. They are the perfect cold treat on a warm summer day.

1½ CUPS ORANGE JUICE
1½ CUPS PLAIN LOW-FAT YOGURT
3 TABLESPOONS HONEY
1 TEASPOON VANILLA EXTRACT

1. In a medium bowl, stir together the orange juice, yogurt, honey, and vanilla until well combined.

2. Pour the mixture into ten 3-ounce ice pop molds. Insert the sticks and freeze for 6 to 8 hours, until thoroughly frozen.

3. To unmold, dip the mold briefly in hot water to easily slide out the ice pops.

Chocolate Shake

PER SERVING:

- ▶ CALORIES: 344
- ▶ FAT (GRAMS): 10.8
- ▶ CHOLESTEROL
(MILLIGRAMS): 20
- ▶ SODIUM (MILLIGRAMS): 332

- ▶ CARBOHYDRATES
(GRAMS): 38.6
- ▶ FIBER (GRAMS): 6.9
- ▶ PROTEIN (GRAMS): 28.1

This high-protein, low-carb drink tastes just like a rich, creamy milk shake. You can substitute almond milk, coconut milk, or regular milk for the soy milk if you like.

1½ CUPS UNSWEETENED SOY MILK

1 SCOOP UNSWEETENED PROTEIN POWDER

3 TABLESPOONS UNSWEETENED COCOA POWDER

13 TO 16 DROPS STEVIA EXTRACT

¹⁄₁₆ TEASPOON XANTHAN GUM

In a blender, add the soy milk, protein powder, cocoa, stevia to taste, and xanthan gum. Process on high speed until well combined, smooth, thick, and creamy. Pour into a large glass and serve immediately.

Cherry and Chocolate Snack Bars

MAKES 16 BARS

PER SERVING:

▶ CALORIES: 109

▶ FAT (GRAMS): 5

▶ CHOLESTEROL
(MILLIGRAMS): 0

▶ SODIUM (MILLIGRAMS): 54

▶ CARBOHYDRATES (GRAMS): 17

▶ FIBER (GRAMS): 1

▶ PROTEIN (GRAMS): 1

These sweet snack bars are chewy, crispy, and sticky all at once. They're a satisfying snack, low in carbs but full of nutrients like magnesium.

2½ CUPS UNSWEETENED PUFFED WHEAT CEREAL

½ CUP CHOPPED PECANS

⅓ CUP ROASTED PUMPKIN SEEDS

¼ CUP COARSELY CHOPPED DRIED CHERRIES

2 TABLESPOONS SESAME SEEDS

1 TABLESPOON FLAXSEED MEAL

½ CUP HONEY

½ TEASPOON VANILLA EXTRACT

⅛ TEASPOON SALT

½ CUP SUGAR-FREE SEMISWEET CHOCOLATE CHIPS

1. Preheat the oven to 300°F. Line an 8-inch square baking pan with a piece of parchment paper long enough to overhang two opposite sides of the pan (to be used to lift the baked bars out later).

2. In a large bowl, add the puffed wheat, pecans, pumpkin seeds, cherries, sesame seeds, and flaxseed meal. Stir to combine.

continued ▶

3. In a small saucepan over medium heat, add the honey, vanilla, and salt, and stir until the mixture is liquid and the salt is dissolved. Drizzle the honey mixture over the cereal mixture and stir until the mixture is well combined.

4. Let cool for several minutes, then add the chocolate chips and stir until they are mixed in. Transfer the mixture to the prepared pan, spreading it evenly and pressing it down with a fork or spatula.

5. Bake until golden brown on top, about 35 minutes. Use a knife to separate the bars from the unlined sides of the pan, set the pan on a wire rack, and let cool to room temperature, about 1 hour.

6. Use the parchment paper to lift the bars out of the pan. Place on a cutting board and cut into 16 bars using a sharp knife. Serve immediately or store in an airtight container at room temperature for up to 1 week.

CHAPTER 6

Soups and Salads

BUTTERNUT SQUASH AND CHIPOTLE SOUP

ROASTED CAULIFLOWER SOUP WITH SMOKED GOUDA

VEGGIE-PACKED MINESTRONE SOUP

CREAMY CHICKEN SOUP WITH ROASTED GARLIC

KALE AND ALMOND SALAD WITH PARMESAN CHEESE
AND LEMON VINAIGRETTE

RADICCHIO, FENNEL, AND ORANGE SALAD WITH
OLIVE VINAIGRETTE

COBB SALAD

STEAK SALAD WITH BLUE CHEESE DRESSING

Butternut Squash and Chipotle Soup

SERVES 6

PER SERVING:

- ▶ CALORIES: 157
- ▶ FAT (GRAMS): 6.5
- ▶ CHOLESTEROL (MILLIGRAMS): 1
- ▶ SODIUM (MILLIGRAMS): 1180
- ▶ CARBOHYDRATES (GRAMS): 18.3
- ▶ FIBER (GRAMS): 2.9
- ▶ PROTEIN (GRAMS): 7.5

Naturally sweet butternut squash, which happens to be a great source of beta carotene, pairs beautifully with the smoky heat of ground chipotle chile. The yogurt garnish has a cooling effect, as well as adding a welcome creaminess to the dish.

2 TABLESPOONS OLIVE OIL

1 SMALL ONION, CHOPPED

2 GARLIC CLOVES, MINCED

1 TEASPOON GROUND CUMIN

1 TEASPOON SALT

¼ TEASPOON PEPPER

¼ TO ½ TEASPOON GROUND CHIPOTLE CHILE

⅛ TEASPOON GROUND CLOVES

1½ POUNDS BUTTERNUT SQUASH (ABOUT 1 MEDIUM SQUASH), PEELED AND CUBED

1 MEDIUM CARROT, DICED

1 STALK CELERY, DICED

6 CUPS VEGETABLE BROTH

½ CUP PLAIN YOGURT, FOR GARNISH

2 TABLESPOONS CHOPPED FRESH CHIVES, FOR GARNISH

1. In a large stockpot over medium-high heat, add the oil and heat it up. Add the onion and garlic and cook, stirring frequently, until softened, about 5 minutes. Stir in the cumin, salt, pepper, chipotle (1/4 teaspoon for some heat, 1/2 teaspoon for more heat), and cloves and cook, stirring, 1 minute more.

2. Add the squash, carrot, celery, and broth and bring to a boil. Reduce the heat to medium-low and simmer, uncovered, until the squash is tender, about 40 minutes.

3. Using an immersion blender, or in batches in a countertop blender, purée the soup. Return the soup to the pot.

4. Heat the soup over medium heat until warmed through. Serve hot, garnished with the yogurt and chives.

Roasted Cauliflower Soup with Smoked Gouda

SERVES 6

PER SERVING:

- ▶ CALORIES: 297
- ▶ FAT (GRAMS): 18.5
- ▶ CHOLESTEROL (MILLIGRAMS): 113
- ▶ SODIUM (MILLIGRAMS): 999
- ▶ CARBOHYDRATES (GRAMS): 12.3
- ▶ FIBER (GRAMS): 3.4
- ▶ PROTEIN (GRAMS): 14.8

This creamy vegetarian soup is enriched with the sweet flavor of caramelized roasted cauliflower. The smokiness of smoked Gouda cheese adds an unexpected twist.

1 HEAD CAULIFLOWER (ABOUT 1½ POUNDS FLORETS), CUT INTO SMALL PIECES

1 MEDIUM ONION, CUT INTO WEDGES

2 TABLESPOONS OLIVE OIL

½ TEASPOON SALT

½ TEASPOON BLACK PEPPER

1 GARLIC CLOVE, MINCED

1 STALK CELERY, FINELY DICED

1 CUP DRY WHITE WINE

4 CUPS VEGETABLE BROTH

¾ CUP HALF-AND-HALF

2 EGG YOLKS, LIGHTLY BEATEN

1 TEASPOON WORCESTERSHIRE SAUCE

¼ TEASPOON CAYENNE PEPPER

6 OUNCES SMOKED GOUDA CHEESE, SHREDDED

2 TABLESPOONS FRESH LEMON JUICE

¼ CUP CHOPPED CHIVES, FOR GARNISH

1. Preheat the oven to 450°F. Place the cauliflower and onion on a large rimmed baking sheet and drizzle with 1 tablespoon of the olive oil. Toss to coat well, then spread out in a single layer. Sprinkle with the salt and black pepper. Roast until tender and beginning to turn brown around the edges, 35 to 45 minutes.

2. While the cauliflower is roasting, in a large lidded saucepan over medium heat, add the remaining 1 tablespoon olive oil. Add the garlic and celery and cook, stirring frequently, until softened, about 2 minutes.

3. Add the wine, cover, and cook for about 5 minutes.

4. Add the broth and the roasted cauliflower and onion and, using an immersion blender or working in batches in a countertop blender, purée the mixture. Heat the soup over medium heat until almost boiling.

5. In a small bowl, whisk together the half-and-half, egg yolks, Worcestershire sauce, and cayenne pepper.

6. Ladle a cup of the hot soup into the cream mixture and whisk to combine, then pour the mixture into the stockpot and stir to mix well. Add the cheese a handful at a time, stirring after each addition and allowing the cheese to melt. Stir in the lemon juice. Do not boil.

7. Serve immediately, garnished with the chives.

Veggie-Packed Minestrone Soup

SERVES 8

PER SERVING:

- CALORIES: 319
- FAT (GRAMS): 7.8
- CHOLESTEROL (MILLIGRAMS): 17
- SODIUM (MILLIGRAMS): 1218
- CARBOHYDRATES (GRAMS): 39.7
- FIBER (GRAMS): 15.5
- PROTEIN (GRAMS): 24.4

This classic Italian soup is loaded with vegetables that deliver vitamins, minerals, and fiber. Cannellini beans give it plenty of protein, too. To make it vegetarian, simply eliminate the bacon, cook the veggies in 2 tablespoons of olive oil, and substitute vegetable broth for the chicken broth. This soup keeps well, so make a big pot and enjoy it all week.

3 OUNCES (ABOUT 3 SLICES) BACON

1 SMALL ONION, FINELY DICED

1 STALK CELERY, DICED

1 MEDIUM CARROT, DICED

OLIVE OIL, IF NEEDED

3 GARLIC CLOVES, MINCED

1 TEASPOON SALT

½ TEASPOON PEPPER

4 CUPS GENTLY PACKED BABY SPINACH OR OTHER DARK LEAFY GREENS

2 MEDIUM ZUCCHINI, DICED

ONE 15-OUNCE CAN DICED TOMATOES AND THEIR JUICE

1 CUP CHOPPED FRESH FLAT-LEAF PARSLEY

6 CUPS CHICKEN BROTH

ONE 15-OUNCE CAN CANNELLINI BEANS, DRAINED AND RINSED

2 OUNCES PARMESAN CHEESE, GRATED

1. In a large stockpot over medium-high heat, cook the bacon until crisp. With tongs, carefully lift the bacon pieces out, reserving the rendered fat in the bottom of the stockpot. Place bacon on paper towels to drain and cool.

2. Add the onion, celery, and carrot to the stockpot (if the bacon fat is not enough, add a bit of olive oil) and cook, stirring frequently, until the vegetables begin to soften, about 5 minutes. Stir in the garlic, salt, and pepper and cook another 2 minutes.

3. Add the spinach, zucchini, tomatoes, parsley, and broth and bring to a boil. Reduce the heat to medium-low and simmer, uncovered, for about 20 minutes.

4. While the soup is simmering, place about half of the beans in a food processor and process until smooth. Add the puréed beans and the whole beans to the soup, and crumble in the bacon strips. Simmer for about fifteen minutes.

5. Serve hot, garnished with Parmesan cheese. Store leftovers in the refrigerator for up to 1 week or in the freezer up to 3 months.

Creamy Chicken Soup with Roasted Garlic

SERVES 6

PER SERVING:

- CALORIES: 381
- FAT (GRAMS): 19.6
- CHOLESTEROL (MILLIGRAMS): 121
- SODIUM (MILLIGRAMS): 1062
- CARBOHYDRATES (GRAMS): 9.9
- FIBER (GRAMS): 0.9
- PROTEIN (GRAMS): 41.5

Garlic is a nutritional powerhouse, providing cardiovascular benefits as well as fighting cancer, bacterial and viral illnesses, and inflammation. Roasting garlic brings out its natural sweetness. This soup combines the deep, complex flavor of roasted garlic with the bite of fresh garlic in a rich, creamy chicken soup that will cure whatever ails you. You won't even miss the noodles.

2 WHOLE HEADS GARLIC (28 CLOVES), CLOVES SEPARATED BUT NOT PEELED

3 TABLESPOONS OLIVE OIL

2 TABLESPOONS UNSALTED BUTTER

1 MEDIUM ONION, THINLY SLICED

2 TEASPOONS MINCED FRESH THYME OR ½ TEASPOON DRIED THYME

4 CUPS CHICKEN BROTH

1 TEASPOON SALT

½ TEASPOON PEPPER

½ CUP HEAVY CREAM

1½ POUNDS COOKED CHICKEN BREAST, CUT INTO BITE-SIZE PIECES

1. Preheat the oven to 400°F.

2. Place 20 of the garlic cloves on a square of aluminum foil, drizzle the olive oil over them, and fold the foil into a sealed packet. Place the foil packet directly on the oven rack and roast until the garlic is soft and golden brown, 45 to 60 minutes.

3. Remove the garlic from the oven, open the foil packet, and let cool. When cool enough to handle, squeeze the garlic cloves out of their papery skins. Peel the remaining 8 garlic cloves.

4. In a large saucepan over medium heat, melt the butter. Add the onion and cook, stirring frequently, until softened, about 5 minutes.

5. Stir in the roasted garlic, fresh garlic, and thyme and until fragrant, about 2 to 3 minutes.

6. Add the broth, salt, and pepper and bring to a boil. Reduce heat to medium-low and simmer for about 20 minutes.

7. Using an immersion blender, or in batches in a countertop blender, purée the soup. Return the soup to the pot, add the cream and chicken, and heat over medium heat until hot.

8. Serve immediately, or cool and store in the refrigerator for up to 1 week.

Kale and Almond Salad with Parmesan Cheese and Lemon Vinaigrette

SERVES 4

PER SERVING:

▶ CALORIES: 283

▶ FAT (GRAMS): 21.8

▶ CHOLESTEROL
(MILLIGRAMS): 15

▶ SODIUM (MILLIGRAMS): 682

▶ CARBOHYDRATES (GRAMS): 14

▶ FIBER (GRAMS): 3.6

▶ PROTEIN (GRAMS): 12.8

Kale is the darling of the nutrition world, and it's not hard to understand why. It's full of calcium; vitamins A, C, and K; copper, potassium, iron, manganese, and phosphorus; plus fiber and antioxidants. Of course, it doesn't hurt that it is also delicious both cooked and raw. Here it gets a simple treatment: a tart lemon vinaigrette, crunchy almonds, and lots of Parmesan cheese.

DRESSING:

1 MEDIUM SHALLOT, MINCED

¼ CUP LEMON JUICE

2 TABLESPOONS CHAMPAGNE VINEGAR

3 TABLESPOONS OLIVE OIL

¾ TEASPOON SALT

½ TEASPOON PEPPER

SALAD:

2 LARGE BUNCHES CURLY KALE, STEMMED AND CUT INTO RIBBONS

½ CUP SLIVERED ALMONDS

1½ CUPS FINELY GRATED PARMESAN CHEESE

For the Dressing:

In a small bowl, combine the minced shallot, lemon juice, vinegar, olive oil, salt, and pepper and whisk until well combined and emulsified.

For the Salad:

In a large salad bowl, toss together the kale and almonds. Drizzle the dressing over the salad, tossing to coat the kale well. Add the Parmesan and toss again gently to distribute it throughout the salad. Serve immediately.

Radicchio, Fennel, and Orange Salad with Olive Vinaigrette

SERVES 4

PER SERVING:

- CALORIES: 129
- FAT (GRAMS): 5.1
- CHOLESTEROL (MILLIGRAMS): 0
- SODIUM (MILLIGRAMS): 601
- CARBOHYDRATES (GRAMS): 20.5
- FIBER (GRAMS): 6.2
- PROTEIN (GRAMS): 3.1

Crunchy fennel bulbs have an exotic flavor reminiscent of licorice, which pairs surprisingly well with tart-sweet oranges and briny olives. Fennel's unique combination of phytonutrients includes a strong anti-inflammatory compound that has been shown to reduce the risk of cancer. Radicchio is a reddish purple-hued leafy green with a pleasing bitter bite.

VINAIGRETTE:

½ TEASPOON ORANGE ZEST

⅓ CUP ORANGE JUICE

¼ CUP APPLE CIDER VINEGAR

¼ CUP PITTED AND CHOPPED KALAMATA OLIVES

1 TABLESPOON MINCED FRESH OREGANO

1 TEASPOON DIJON MUSTARD

¾ TEASPOON SALT

½ TEASPOON PEPPER

1 TABLESPOON OLIVE OIL

SALAD:

3 HEADS RADICCHIO, TORN INTO BITE-SIZE PIECES

2 MEDIUM FENNEL BULBS, TRIMMED AND THINLY SLICED

1 LARGE ORANGE (SUCH AS VALENCIA OR NAVEL)

For the dressing:

In a small bowl, whisk together the orange zest, orange juice, vinegar, olives, oregano, mustard, salt, and pepper. Whisk in the oil.

For the salad:

1. In a large salad bowl, toss the radicchio and fennel together.

2. Peel the orange with a sharp knife, making sure to remove all the white pith. Quarter the orange, and thinly slice each quarter crosswise. Add the orange slices to the salad bowl and toss to combine.

3. Drizzle the dressing over the salad and toss to coat well. Serve immediately.

Cobb Salad

SERVES 4

PER SERVING:

▶ CALORIES: 451

▶ FAT (GRAMS): 33.7

▶ CHOLESTEROL
(MILLIGRAMS): 160

▶ SODIUM (MILLIGRAMS): 945

▶ CARBOHYDRATES (GRAMS): 9

▶ FIBER (GRAMS): 4

▶ PROTEIN (GRAMS): 29.5

Cobb salad is loaded with protein—from the chicken, bacon, blue cheese, and hard-boiled eggs—making it a satisfying meal-size salad. Fortunately, it also has lots of nutritious veggies, fiber, and healthy fats.

DRESSING:

¼ CUP RED WINE VINEGAR

1 SMALL SHALLOT, MINCED

1 TABLESPOON FRESH LEMON JUICE

2 TEASPOONS DIJON MUSTARD

¾ TEASPOON SALT

½ TEASPOON PEPPER

PINCH OF SUGAR

⅓ CUP OLIVE OIL

SALAD:

1 LARGE HEAD ROMAINE LETTUCE, CHOPPED

8 OUNCES COOKED CHICKEN BREAST, DICED OR SHREDDED

2 LARGE EGGS, HARD-BOILED, PEELED, AND CHOPPED

2 MEDIUM TOMATOES, DICED

1 LARGE CUCUMBER, PEELED, SEEDED, AND SLICED

½ AVOCADO, DICED

2 SLICES COOKED BACON, CRUMBLED

2 OUNCES BLUE CHEESE, CRUMBLED

For the dressing:

In a small bowl, whisk together the vinegar, shallot, lemon juice, mustard, salt, pepper, and sugar in a small bowl until well combined. Whisk in the olive oil.

For the salad:

1. Put the lettuce in a large mixing bowl and drizzle with half the dressing. Toss to coat. Arrange the lettuce on four serving plates. Artfully top with the chicken, eggs, tomatoes, cucumber, avocado, bacon, and blue cheese.

2. Drizzle the remaining dressing over the salads and serve immediately.

Steak Salad with Blue Cheese Dressing

SERVES 4

PER SERVING:

- CALORIES: 346
- FAT (GRAMS): 20.6
- CHOLESTEROL
  (MILLIGRAMS): 71
- SODIUM (MILLIGRAMS): 818
- CARBOHYDRATES (GRAMS): 3.6
- FIBER (GRAMS): 0.7
- PROTEIN (GRAMS): 35.5

Flank steak is a lean cut of beef that is perfect for grilling. This quick, easy salad delivers lots of flavor, protein, and iron, making it hearty and satisfying enough to be a meal in and of itself. The classic steak and blue cheese combination is sure to satisfy big appetites.

ONE 1-POUND FLANK STEAK, TRIMMED

1 TABLESPOON OLIVE OIL

1 TEASPOON SALT

½ TEASPOON PEPPER

¾ CUP WELL-SHAKEN BUTTERMILK

¼ CUP CRUMBLED BLUE CHEESE

½ TEASPOON WORCESTERSHIRE SAUCE

⅛ TEASPOON HOT PEPPER SAUCE

4 SMALL HEADS BIBB LETTUCE, HALVED LENGTHWISE,
    OR 2 SMALL HEADS BOSTON LETTUCE, QUARTERED LENGTHWISE

¼ CUP COARSELY CHOPPED TOASTED PECANS

2 TABLESPOONS MINCED FRESH CHIVES

1. Preheat a grill or barbecue to medium-high heat.

2. Brush the steak on both sides with the olive oil, and sprinkle with ¾ teaspoon of the salt and the ½ teaspoon pepper.

3. Grill the steak, turning once, until the desired degree of doneness has been achieved, about 8 minutes per side for medium rare. Transfer the steak to a cutting board and let rest for 10 minutes.

4. To make the dressing, in a small bowl, stir together the buttermilk, blue cheese, Worcestershire sauce, hot pepper sauce, and the remaining 1/4 teaspoon salt.

5. Cut the meat into 1/4-inch-thick slices, cutting across the grain.

6. Arrange the lettuce on four salad plates, dividing it equally. Arrange the steak on top of the lettuce. Drizzle the dressing over the top and sprinkle with the pecans.

7. Serve immediately, garnished with chives.

CHAPTER 7

Entrées

PIZZA MARGHERITA WITH A CAULIFLOWER CRUST

QUINOA AND VEGETABLE GRATIN

GARLIC-LIME SHRIMP AND PEPPERS

SEARED TROUT WITH CHERRY TOMATOES AND BACON

ROASTED SALMON WITH CARAMELIZED LEEKS

SEARED CHICKEN VERACRUZ

PROSCIUTTO-WRAPPED CHICKEN STUFFED WITH GOAT CHEESE

LEMON-ROSEMARY SEARED STEAK WITH ASPARAGUS AND MUSHROOMS

Pizza Margherita with a Cauliflower Crust

SERVES 4

PER SERVING:

- ▶ CALORIES: 312
- ▶ FAT (GRAMS): 23.4
- ▶ CHOLESTEROL (MILLIGRAMS): 58
- ▶ SODIUM (MILLIGRAMS): 1,475
- ▶ CARBOHYDRATES (GRAMS): 16.9
- ▶ FIBER (GRAMS): 6
- ▶ PROTEIN (GRAMS): 13.5

Thought you said farewell to pizza when you went low-carb? Think again. This grain-free pizza, on a crust made out of cauliflower, will rock your world. Here it gets a simple treatment with a quick tomato sauce, cheese, and fresh basil, but you can top it with any of your favorite pizza toppings. The instructions may seem long and intimidating, but rest assured, the whole thing is quick and easy to make.

CRUST:

1 MEDIUM HEAD CAULIFLOWER, STEM TRIMMED
    AND CUT INTO SMALL FLORETS

2 TABLESPOONS ALMOND MEAL

1 TABLESPOON OLIVE OIL

½ TEASPOON DRIED BASIL

½ TEASPOON DRIED OREGANO

½ TEASPOON SALT

1 LARGE EGG, LIGHTLY BEATEN

COOKING SPRAY

SAUCE:

2 TABLESPOONS OLIVE OIL

¼ MEDIUM ONION, DICED

3 GARLIC CLOVES, MINCED

ONE 28-OUNCE CAN DICED TOMATOES IN JUICE

1 TABLESPOON MINCED FRESH BASIL

1½ TEASPOONS SALT

½ TEASPOON PEPPER

TOPPINGS:

3 OUNCES FRESH MOZZARELLA, THINLY SLICED

½ TEASPOON SALT

¼ TEASPOON PEPPER

6 TO 8 LARGE BASIL LEAVES, JULIENNED

For the Crust:

1. Place a pizza stone or rimmed baking sheet in the oven and preheat it to 450°F.

2. Put the cauliflower in a food processor and pulse until it is in fine crumbs and looks a bit like snow. Transfer to a microwave-safe bowl, cover, and microwave on high for 4 minutes. Let cool. Transfer the cooked cauliflower to a clean dish towel and squeeze as much water out of it as you can.

3. In a medium bowl, combine the drained cauliflower with the almond meal, olive oil, basil, oregano, and salt. Toss together, then add the egg and mix well.

4. Place a piece of parchment paper on the counter and spray it with cooking spray. Turn the dough out onto the prepared parchment paper and, using your hands, pat it out into a 10-inch round pizza crust.

5. Using the parchment paper, transfer the crust onto the heated pizza stone or baking sheet. Bake until the crust begins to turn golden, about 10 minutes. Remove from the oven.

For the Sauce:

1. In a medium lidded saucepan over medium-high heat, heat the oil. Add the onion and garlic and cook, stirring, until softened, about 5 minutes. Stir in the tomatoes, basil, salt, and pepper and bring to a boil. Reduce heat to medium-low, cover, and simmer for 10 minutes.

2. Spoon several spoonfuls of sauce onto the pizza crust and spread into an even layer with the back of the spoon, spreading it all the way to the edges of the crust.

continued ▶

Pizza Margherita with a Cauliflower Crust *continued* ▶

For the Toppings:

Top the pizza with the cheese. Sprinkle the salt and pepper over the top. Bake until the cheese is bubbly and beginning to brown, about 15 minutes. Let cool for 2 minutes, then garnish with the basil leaves, cut the pizza into wedges, and serve.

Quinoa and Vegetable Gratin

SERVES 6

PER SERVING:

▶ CALORIES: 296

▶ FAT (GRAMS): 13.7

▶ CHOLESTEROL
(MILLIGRAMS): 108

▶ SODIUM (MILLIGRAMS): 492

▶ CARBOHYDRATES
(GRAMS): 29.7

▶ FIBER (GRAMS): 4.5

▶ PROTEIN (GRAMS): 13.8

This light vegetarian entrée highlights the best of summer produce—ripe toma-toes, bright yellow squash, earthy red onions, and fresh herbs, all melded with a light but flavorful cheese sauce.

COOKING SPRAY

5 TEASPOONS OLIVE OIL

2 MEDIUM RED ONIONS, CHOPPED

1 LARGE RED BELL PEPPER, SEEDED AND CHOPPED

1 POUND YELLOW SQUASH, CUT INTO ¼-INCH-THICK SLICES

2 GARLIC CLOVES, MINCED

¾ CUP COOKED QUINOA

½ CUP THINLY SLICED FRESH BASIL

1½ TEASPOONS CHOPPED FRESH THYME

¾ TEASPOON SALT

½ TEASPOON PEPPER

½ CUP 2% MILK

¾ CUP (ABOUT 3 OUNCES) AGED GRUYÈRE CHEESE, SHREDDED

3 EGGS, LIGHTLY BEATEN

1 LARGE TOMATO, CUT INTO 8 SLICES

½ CUP WHOLE-WHEAT BREAD CRUMBS

continued ▶

1. Preheat the oven to 375°F. Coat an 11-by-7-inch baking dish with cooking spray.

2. In a large skillet over medium-high heat, heat the olive oil. Add the onions and cook, stirring, until they begin to soften, about 3 minutes. Add the bell pepper and cook for about 2 minutes more. Stir in the squash and garlic and continue to cook, stirring occasionally, for about 5 minutes more.

3. Transfer the hot vegetable mixture to a large bowl and add the quinoa, ¼ cup of the basil, the thyme, ½ teaspoon of the salt, and the pepper.

4. In a medium bowl, whisk together the remaining ¼ teaspoon salt, the milk, Gruyère cheese, and eggs. Pour over the vegetable mixture in the bowl. Stir to mix.

5. Transfer the vegetable-egg mixture to the prepared baking dish and lay the tomato slices on top in a single layer. Cover with the bread crumbs, spritz with a little cooking spray, and bake until the topping is nicely browned, about 40 minutes.

6. Serve hot, garnished with the remaining basil.

Garlic-Lime Shrimp and Peppers

SERVES 4

PER SERVING:

▶ CALORIES: 384

▶ FAT (GRAMS): 14

▶ CHOLESTEROL
(MILLIGRAMS): 478

▶ SODIUM (MILLIGRAMS): 847

▶ CARBOHYDRATES (GRAMS): 9

▶ FIBER (GRAMS): 1

▶ PROTEIN (GRAMS): 52.1

With succulent prawns and crisp-tender veggies, this is the perfect quick dish for a weeknight meal.

JUICE AND ZEST OF ONE LIME

4 TABLESPOONS OLIVE OIL, DIVIDED

3 GARLIC CLOVES, MINCED

1 TEASPOON SEA SALT, DIVIDED

¼ CUP CHOPPED, FRESH CILANTRO PLUS EXTRA FOR GARNISH

2 POUNDS LARGE SHRIMP, PEELED AND DEVEINED

1 RED ONION, THINLY SLICED

1 BELL PEPPER, ANY COLOR, SLICED

¼ TEASPOON FRESHLY GROUND BLACK PEPPER

1. In a large nonreactive bowl, whisk together the lime juice and zest, two tablespoons of the olive oil, the garlic, ½ teaspoon of the salt, and the cilantro. Toss with the shrimp. Marinate for 10 minutes.

2. In a large, heavy skillet set over medium-high heat, heat the remaining two tablespoons of olive oil. Add the red onion and bell pepper. Cook, stirring occasionally, until the vegetables are crisp-tender, about four minutes.

3. Remove the shrimp from the marinade and add to the vegetables along with the black pepper and the remaining ½ teaspoon of sea salt. Cook, stirring occasionally, until the shrimp are pink, about five minutes more.

4. Garnish with cilantro and lime wedges.

Seared Trout with Cherry Tomatoes and Bacon

SERVES 4

PER SERVING:

▶ CALORIES: 383

▶ FAT (GRAMS): 17.7

▶ CHOLESTEROL
(MILLIGRAMS): 134

▶ SODIUM (MILLIGRAMS): 1446

▶ CARBOHYDRATES (GRAMS): 4.7

▶ FIBER (GRAMS): 1.5

▶ PROTEIN (GRAMS): 48.9

In this dish, you get lots of protein and the heart-healthy benefits of the fish, plus the mouthwatering flavor of smoky bacon. Serve this with oven-roasted Brussels sprouts for a satisfying meal.

4 SLICES BACON

1 PINT CHERRY TOMATOES, HALVED

1 GARLIC CLOVE, MINCED

1 TEASPOON SALT

1 TEASPOON PEPPER

1 TABLESPOON MINCED FRESH THYME

COOKING SPRAY

FOUR 6-OUNCE TROUT FILLETS

4 LEMON WEDGES

1. In a medium skillet over medium-high heat, add the bacon and cook, turning once, until crisp, about 5 to 7 minutes. Transfer the bacon strips to a paper-towel-lined plate to drain, then crumble. Drain off all but about 1 tablespoon of the bacon fat from the skillet.

2. To the bacon fat in the skillet, add the cherry tomatoes, garlic, ½ teaspoon of the salt, and ½ teaspoon of the pepper and cook, stirring, until the tomatoes just begin to break down, about 3 minutes. Remove from the heat and stir in the crumbled bacon and thyme.

3. Coat a large nonstick skillet with cooking spray and heat it over medium-high heat. Sprinkle the fish fillets with the remaining ½ teaspoon salt and ½ teaspoon pepper and add them to the pan (you may need to cook the fish in two batches to avoid overcrowding).

4. Cook the fish, turning once, until it is cooked through and flakes easily with a fork, 2 to 3 minutes per side.

5. Transfer the fish fillets to serving plates, and serve topped with the tomato mixture and with lemon wedges alongside.

Roasted Salmon with Caramelized Leeks

SERVES 4

PER SERVING:

- ▶ CALORIES: 378
- ▶ FAT (GRAMS): 21.2
- ▶ CHOLESTEROL (MILLIGRAMS): 107

- ▶ SODIUM (MILLIGRAMS): 404
- ▶ CARBOHYDRATES (GRAMS): 6.4
- ▶ FIBER (GRAMS): 1
- ▶ PROTEIN (GRAMS): 38.3

Salmon is full of super-healthy omega-3 fatty acids. Omega-3s provide many health benefits, protecting the body from cardiovascular disease and joint problems, improving mood and cognition, and reducing cancer risk. In this extremely simple dish, flaky roasted salmon is topped with luscious slow-cooked caramelized leeks. Serve it alongside green beans or broccoli for a quick and easy meal.

COOKING SPRAY

1 TABLESPOON BUTTER

2 LEEKS, TRIMMED, HALVED LENGTHWISE, THINLY SLICED, RINSED, AND DRIED

½ TEASPOON SALT

½ TEASPOON FRESH LEMON JUICE

FOUR 6-OUNCE SALMON FILLETS

¼ TEASPOON BLACK PEPPER

⅛ TEASPOON CAYENNE PEPPER

1. Preheat the oven to 400°F. Coat a large rimmed baking sheet with cooking spray.

2. In a large nonstick skillet over medium heat, add the butter and leeks and cook, stirring occasionally, until the leeks are softened, about 5 minutes. Stir in ¼ teaspoon of the salt, and reduce the heat to low. Cook about 20 minutes more, stirring occasionally, until the leeks are browned and very soft. Remove the pan from the heat and stir in the lemon juice.

3. Place the salmon on the prepared baking sheet and season with the remaining ¼ teaspoon salt, black pepper, and cayenne pepper. Roast the salmon until it is cooked through and flakes easily with a fork, 8 to 10 minutes.

4. Serve the salmon topped with the caramelized leeks.

Seared Chicken Veracruz

SERVES 4

PER SERVING:

▶ CALORIES: 443

▶ FAT (GRAMS): 17.9

▶ CHOLESTEROL
(MILLIGRAMS): 128

▶ SODIUM (MILLIGRAMS): 897

▶ CARBOHYDRATES
(GRAMS): 10.2

▶ FIBER (GRAMS): 2.5

▶ PROTEIN (GRAMS): 48.2

This easy chicken dish from the Mexican state of Veracruz gets its flavor from tomatoes, garlic, chiles, and olives. Serve it alongside zucchini roasted with garlic and pumpkin seeds.

1 TABLESPOON OLIVE OIL

1 TEASPOON DRIED OREGANO

1 TEASPOON SALT

4 SKIN-ON, BONE-IN CHICKEN BREAST HALVES (ABOUT 1½ POUNDS)

3 MEDIUM TOMATOES, DICED

1 MEDIUM ONION, HALVED AND THINLY SLICED

2 JALAPEÑO PEPPERS, SEEDED AND VERY THINLY SLICED

4 GARLIC CLOVES, MINCED

¼ CUP THINLY SLICED PITTED GREEN OLIVES

1 CUP DRY WHITE WINE

1 LIME, CUT INTO 4 WEDGES

1. In a large lidded skillet over high heat, heat the oil. Sprinkle the oregano and ½ teaspoon of the salt over the chicken and add the chicken to the pan. Cook, turning once or twice, until it is browned on all sides, about 10 minutes.

2. Add the tomatoes, onion, jalapeños, garlic, and olives, scattering them over the chicken. Cook until the vegetables begin to soften, about 5 minutes.

3. Add the remaining ½ teaspoon salt and the wine and bring to a boil. Reduce the heat to medium-low, cover, and simmer for about 10 minutes, until the chicken is thoroughly cooked and the vegetables are tender.

4. Serve the chicken hot, topped with the sauce, with lime wedges on the side.

Prosciutto-Wrapped Chicken Stuffed with Goat Cheese

SERVES 4

PER SERVING:

▶ CALORIES: 416

▶ FAT (GRAMS): 18.5

▶ CHOLESTEROL
(MILLIGRAMS): 164

▶ SODIUM (MILLIGRAMS): 769

▶ CARBOHYDRATES (GRAMS): 0.8

▶ FIBER (GRAMS): 0

▶ PROTEIN (GRAMS): 60.6

This simple chicken dish is elegant enough to serve to company. A crisp green salad with a tart vinaigrette nicely completes the meal.

2 OUNCES GOAT CHEESE

1 TEASPOON DRIED BASIL

1 TEASPOON DRIED OREGANO

4 BONELESS, SKINLESS CHICKEN BREAST HALVES

¾ TEASPOON SALT

½ TEASPOON PEPPER

4 SLICES PROSCIUTTO

2 TABLESPOONS OLIVE OIL

1. Preheat the oven to 375°F.

2. In a small bowl, stir together the goat cheese, basil, and oregano.

3. Place a chicken breast between two sheet of plastic wrap or waxed paper and pound it to about ¼- to ½-inch thick. Repeat for the remaining 3 chicken breasts.

4. Divide the goat cheese mixture evenly among the pieces of chicken, spreading it in a strip down the middle. Roll the chicken around the goat cheese and season with salt and pepper. Wrap each chicken roll in a piece of prosciutto and use a toothpick to secure.

continued ▶

5. In an oven-safe skillet over medium-high heat, add the oil. When the oil is very hot, add the chicken rolls and cook, turning occasionally, until the chicken is browned on all sides, 6 to 8 minutes.

6. Transfer the skillet to oven and bake until cooked through, about 15 minutes.

7. Remove from the oven and let rest for a few minutes, then slice each chicken roll into several pieces and serve immediately.

Lemon-Rosemary Seared Steak with Asparagus and Mushrooms

SERVES 4

PER SERVING:

▶ CALORIES: 458

▶ FAT (GRAMS): 21.6

▶ CHOLESTEROL (MILLIGRAMS): 94

▶ SODIUM (MILLIGRAMS): 687

▶ CARBOHYDRATES (GRAMS): 12.3

▶ FIBER (GRAMS): 3.8

▶ PROTEIN (GRAMS): 53.1

It doesn't get much simpler—or more elegant—than seared steak with sautéed asparagus and mushrooms. The refined flavors of lemon zest, rosemary, and garlic make the dish shine.

1½ POUNDS FLANK STEAK, 1 INCH THICK

4 GARLIC CLOVES, MINCED

1 TABLESPOON FRESH ROSEMARY, MINCED

1 TEASPOON SALT

½ TEASPOON PEPPER

2 TABLESPOONS OLIVE OIL

1 SMALL ONION, THINLY SLICED LENGTHWISE

1 POUND ASPARAGUS, TRIMMED AND CUT INTO 2-INCH PIECES

1 POUND BUTTON OR CREMINI MUSHROOMS, SLICED

1 TEASPOON GRATED FRESH LEMON ZEST

1. Using a sharp knife, make ⅛-inch-deep cuts in the steak in a diamond pattern on both sides. Spread half of the garlic and half of the rosemary on the steak on both sides, and then sprinkle with ½ teaspoon of the salt and ¼ teaspoon of the pepper.

continued ▶

2. In a large skillet over medium-high heat, add 1 tablespoon of the olive oil. When the oil is very hot, add steak and cook it about 4 minutes per side (longer if you prefer it cooked more than medium-rare). Transfer the steak to a cutting board, cover with foil, and let rest for at least 5 minutes.

3. Heat the remaining 1 tablespoon of the olive oil in the skillet and add the onion. Cook, stirring frequently, until the onion begins to soften, about 3 minutes. Add the remaining garlic and cook 1 or 2 minutes more. Stir in the asparagus, mushrooms, and the remaining $\frac{1}{2}$ teaspoon salt and $\frac{1}{4}$ teaspoon pepper and cook, stirring frequently, for about 5 minutes, until the mushrooms are soft and the asparagus is crisp-tender. Add the lemon zest and the remaining rosemary, and stir to combine. Stir and cook for 1 more minute.

4. To serve, slice the steak across the grain into $\frac{1}{8}$-inch-thick slices and serve with the vegetables.

Desserts

BANANA-CHOCOLATE—PEANUT BUTTER "ICE CREAM"

CHOCOLATE AND VANILLA MERINGUE SWIRLS

CINNAMON-PECAN THINS

HONEY-BLUEBERRY TART

NUT-CRUSTED MINI MAPLE CHEESECAKES

CARROT CAKE WITH WHIPPED COCONUT CREAM FROSTING

CHOCOLATE-FILLED STRAWBERRY SOUFFLÉS

FROSTED BROWNIES

Banana-Chocolate–Peanut Butter "Ice Cream"

SERVES 4

PER SERVING:

▶ CALORIES: 156

▶ FAT (GRAMS): 4.6

▶ CHOLESTEROL
(MILLIGRAMS): 0

▶ SODIUM (MILLIGRAMS): 1

▶ CARBOHYDRATES (GRAMS): 29

▶ FIBER (GRAMS): 3.9

▶ PROTEIN (GRAMS): 3.5

All you need is a food processor or blender, a freezer, and a bit of patience to make this delicious frozen treat. Made with bananas, peanut butter, and cocoa, it's sure to be a crowd-pleaser.

4 VERY RIPE BANANAS, PEELED AND DICED

2 TABLESPOONS ALL-NATURAL,
    NO-SUGAR-ADDED, CREAMY PEANUT BUTTER

2 TEASPOONS UNSWEETENED COCOA POWDER

½ TEASPOON VANILLA EXTRACT

15 DROPS LIQUID STEVIA EXTRACT

1. Place the diced bananas in a bowl and freeze for at least 1 hour, until they are thoroughly frozen.

2. Transfer the bananas to a food processor and process until smooth. Add the peanut butter, cocoa powder, vanilla, and stevia and process until well combined.

3. Transfer the mixture to a container with a lid and freeze for 1 or 2 hours. Let sit on the countertop for about 5 minutes before serving. Serve cold.

Chocolate and Vanilla Meringue Swirls

MAKES ABOUT 48 COOKIES (6 COOKIES PER SERVING)

PER SERVING:

- CALORIES: 45
- FAT (GRAMS): 0.1
- CHOLESTEROL (MILLIGRAMS): 0
- SODIUM (MILLIGRAMS): 21
- CARBOHYDRATES (GRAMS): 9.7
- FIBER (GRAMS): 0
- PROTEIN (GRAMS): 1.5

These adorable little meringue swirls are made with real sugar, but they are so light and airy that a serving of six bite-size treats contains fewer than 10 grams of carbs. If you don't have pastry bags, you can use heavy-duty resealable plastic bags. Before filling, snip a hole in one corner of each bag and insert a pastry tip.

2 TABLESPOONS CONFECTIONERS' SUGAR

1 TABLESPOON UNSWEETENED COCOA POWDER

¼ CUP GRANULATED SUGAR

1 TABLESPOON CORNSTARCH

3 EGG WHITES, AT ROOM TEMPERATURE

1 TEASPOON VANILLA EXTRACT

¼ TEASPOON CREAM OF TARTAR

1. Preheat the oven to 300°F. Line two baking sheets with parchment paper.

2. In a small bowl, combine the confectioners' sugar and cocoa.

3. In a separate small bowl, combine the granulated sugar and cornstarch.

4. In a clean, large mixing bowl using an electric mixer set on medium-high speed, beat together the egg whites, vanilla, and cream of tartar. With the mixer running, slowly add the sugar-starch mixture a spoonful at a time. Continue to beat until the mixture forms stiff peaks.

continued ▶

5. Transfer half of the mixture to a separate bowl.

6. Gently fold the cocoa mixture into one of the bowls of the egg white mixture.

7. Spoon the chocolate and plain meringue mixtures into two separate pastry bags fitted with ½-inch star-shaped tips. Pipe 24 chocolate swirls, each about 1 inch in diameter, onto the prepared baking sheets. Next, pipe white swirls the same size on top of the chocolate swirls. Repeat with the remaining meringue mixtures, reversing the order (white on the bottom, chocolate on top) for another 24 swirls (you'll have to bake in at least two batches).

8. Bake for 10 minutes. Turn the oven off, but leave the baking sheets inside. Let the meringues sit in the closed, turned-off oven for another 30 minutes or so, until they are dry and crisp.

Cinnamon-Pecan Thins

MAKES ABOUT 48 COOKIES (2 COOKIES PER SERVING)

PER SERVING:

▶ CALORIES: 106

▶ FAT (GRAMS): 7.3

▶ CHOLESTEROL
(MILLIGRAMS): 17

▶ SODIUM (MILLIGRAMS): 54

▶ CARBOHYDRATES (GRAMS): 9.4

▶ FIBER (GRAMS): 0.7

▶ PROTEIN (GRAMS): 1.4

These crisp, crunchy cookies are flavored with spicy cinnamon and toasty pecans. Whole-wheat flour keeps them on the healthful side. A combination of noncaloric sweetener and sugar ensures delicious flavor.

1¼ CUPS WHOLE-WHEAT PASTRY FLOUR

1 TEASPOON BAKING POWDER

¼ TEASPOON SALT

½ CUP UNSALTED BUTTER (1 STICK)

½ CUP NONCALORIC GRANULATED SWEETENER (LIKE SPLENDA)

¼ CUP PACKED LIGHT BROWN SUGAR

1 EGG

1 TEASPOON VANILLA EXTRACT

1 CUP FINELY CHOPPED PECANS

¼ CUP GRANULATED SUGAR

1½ TEASPOONS GROUND CINNAMON

1. In a medium mixing bowl, combine the flour, baking powder, and salt.

2. In a large mixing bowl with an electric mixer set on medium-high, cream together the butter, sweetener, and brown sugar. Add the egg and vanilla and beat until well blended.

3. Add the flour mixture to the butter mixture and beat on low until incorporated. Stir in the pecans with a spoon.

continued ▶

4. Divide the dough and form each half into a 6-inch cylinder. Wrap snugly in plastic wrap and chill thoroughly in the refrigerator or freezer, 1 to 2 hours.

5. Preheat the oven to 350°F.

6. Let the chilled dough stand at room temperature for 5 minutes. In a small bowl, stir together the granulated sugar and cinnamon, then spread the mixture out on a plate. Roll the dough logs in the cinnamon-sugar mixture to thoroughly coat the outside.

7. Slice each log into 24 ¼-inch-thick rounds (you should get about 48 cookies total). Arrange the cookies about 2½ inches apart on an ungreased baking sheet (you'll have to bake in at least two batches), and bake until lightly browned for 10 to 12 minutes. Cool the cookies on a wire rack.

Honey-Blueberry Tart

SERVES 12

PER SERVING:

▶ CALORIES: 196

▶ FAT (GRAMS): 13.5

▶ CHOLESTEROL

(MILLIGRAMS): 25

▶ SODIUM (MILLIGRAMS): 99

▶ CARBOHYDRATES

(GRAMS): 17.2

▶ FIBER (GRAMS): 1.3

▶ PROTEIN (GRAMS): 3.7

Blueberries are considered true superstars of the nutrition world. They are low in calories and carbohydrates but extremely high in antioxidants. Here they star in a cream-filled, graham cracker–crusted tart that's sweetened with a touch of honey.

CRUST:

½ CUP WALNUTS, LIGHTLY TOASTED (SEE TIP)

6 SHEETS WHOLE-WHEAT GRAHAM CRACKERS, BROKEN UP

1 EGG WHITE

1 TABLESPOON UNSALTED BUTTER, MELTED

1 TABLESPOON CANOLA OIL

PINCH OF SALT

FILLING:

8 OUNCES REDUCED-FAT CREAM CHEESE, AT ROOM TEMPERATURE

¼ CUP REDUCED-FAT SOUR CREAM

¼ CUP HONEY, PLUS 2 TABLESPOONS

2 CUPS FRESH BLUEBERRIES

Preheat the oven to 325°F.

For the Crust:

1. Put the walnuts in a food processor and pulse to coarsely chop. Add the graham crackers and process until ground to fine crumbs.

continued ▶

2. In a medium bowl, whisk the egg white until frothy. Add the walnut–graham cracker mixture, butter, oil, and salt and stir to moisten the crumbs thoroughly.

3. With your hands, press the mixture into the bottom and about 1/2 inch up the sides of an ungreased 9-inch tart pan.

4. Place the tart pan on top of a baking sheet and bake the crust until it is very dry and beginning to brown around the edges, about 8 minutes. Place the crust, still in the tart pan, on a wire rack to cool.

For the Filling:

1. In a medium bowl using an electric mixer set on low, beat together the cream cheese, sour cream, and 1/4 cup of the honey.

2. When the crust is thoroughly cooled, carefully spread the cream cheese mixture evenly over the bottom. Arrange the blueberries in a single layer on top of the cream cheese filling. Drizzle the remaining 2 tablespoons honey over the tart and chill in the refrigerator until firm, at least 1 hour. Cut into wedges to serve.

Tip: To toast the walnuts, heat a skillet over medium-high heat. When the pan is hot, add the nuts, spreading them out in a single layer. Cook, stirring frequently, until the nuts turn golden brown and become fragrant, about 10 minutes. Immediately remove the nuts from the hot pan to stop the cooking.

Nut-Crusted Mini Maple Cheesecakes

PER SERVING:

▶ CALORIES: 271

▶ FAT (GRAMS): 21.5

▶ CHOLESTEROL (MILLIGRAMS): 80

▶ SODIUM (MILLIGRAMS): 154

▶ CARBOHYDRATES (GRAMS): 10.8

▶ FIBER (GRAMS): 0.6

▶ PROTEIN (GRAMS): 10.3

These cute little treats combine the homey flavors of nuts and maple syrup in a rich, velvety cheesecake that you get to have all to yourself. If you can't find maple extract, substitute vanilla. The cheesecakes will have a more subtle maple flavor, but they'll still be delicious.

CRUST:

¾ CUP FINELY MINCED NUTS (WALNUTS, MACADAMIA NUTS, PECANS, ALMONDS, OR A COMBINATION)

¼ CUP VANILLA PROTEIN POWDER

3 TABLESPOONS UNSALTED BUTTER, MELTED

FILLING:

1 POUND CREAM CHEESE, AT ROOM TEMPERATURE

½ CUP MAPLE SYRUP

1 TEASPOON MAPLE EXTRACT

PINCH OF SALT

2 LARGE EGGS, LIGHTLY BEATEN

Line the cups of a standard 12-cup muffin tin with 12 foil liners.

continued ▶

For the Crust:

1. Combine the nuts, protein powder, and butter in a food processor and process until it begins to stick together.

2. Spoon 1 heaped tablespoon of the crust mixture into 1 cup of the prepared muffin tin, and press into the bottom of the liner. Repeat for the remaining 11 cups of the muffin tin. Place the pan in the freezer to chill for about 30 minutes.

For the Filling:

1. Combine the cream cheese, maple syrup, maple extract, and salt in a large bowl and mix to blend. Add the eggs and stir until incorporated.

2. Preheat the oven to 325°F.

3. Spoon the filling into the crusts, dividing evenly. Each liner should be about three-fourths full.

4. Bake for 25 minutes. Cool completely on a rack. Serve at room temperature or chilled.

Carrot Cake with Whipped Coconut Cream Frosting

SERVES 12

PER SERVING:

▶ CALORIES: 294

▶ FAT (GRAMS): 22.4

▶ CHOLESTEROL
(MILLIGRAMS): 77

▶ SODIUM (MILLIGRAMS): 353

▶ CARBOHYDRATES
(GRAMS): 20.3

▶ FIBER (GRAMS): 3.1

▶ PROTEIN (GRAMS): 7.5

A cake that's packed with carrots has to be healthy, right? While that may not always be true, in this case, this nutritious cake recipe is a winner. This grain-free cake is made with shredded carrot, sweetened with just a touch of honey or agave nectar, and spiced with cinnamon and nutmeg. If you can't find coconut cream, substitute a 15-ounce can of full-fat coconut milk. After chilling the can overnight, flip it over, open it, then pour off the thin liquid (and reserve for another use), retaining only the thick cream that will be underneath it.

CAKE:

COOKING SPRAY

3 CUPS ALMOND MEAL

1 TEASPOON SALT

1 TEASPOON BAKING SODA

1 TEASPOON GROUND CINNAMON

1 TEASPOON GROUND NUTMEG

5 EGGS

½ CUP HONEY OR AGAVE NECTAR

¼ CUP COCONUT OR CANOLA OIL

3 CUPS GRATED CARROTS

1 CUP FINELY CHOPPED WALNUTS

FROSTING:

1 CUP UNSWEETENED COCONUT CREAM, CHILLED OVERNIGHT

continued ▶

1 TABLESPOON HONEY OR AGAVE NECTAR

½ TEASPOON VANILLA EXTRACT

½ CUP UNSWEETENED FLAKED COCONUT, TOASTED (SEE TIP),
    FOR GARNISH (OPTIONAL)

Preheat the oven to 350°F. Coat the interior of two 9-inch round cake pans with cooking spray.

For the Cake:

1. In a large bowl, combine the almond meal, salt, baking soda, cinnamon, and nutmeg.

2. In a medium bowl, whisk together the eggs, honey or agave nectar, and oil. Add the carrots and walnuts and stir to combine.

3. Mix the egg mixture into the almond meal mixture until incorporated.

4. Transfer the batter to the prepared baking pans, dividing evenly. Bake until a toothpick inserted into the center of the cakes comes out clean, 30 to 35 minutes.

5. Remove from the oven and let cool in the pans for about 5 minutes, then invert onto a wire rack to cool completely.

For the Frosting:

1. In a large mixing bowl using an electric mixer set on high, add the coconut cream and beat until light and fluffy, about 5 minutes. Add the honey and the vanilla and beat to incorporate.

2. To assemble the cake, lay one layer, top-side down, on a cake plate. Spread frosting with a spatula to cover the top well. Place the second layer on top of the first, top-side up. Spread frosting to cover the top of the cake, then the sides. Top with the toasted coconut flakes, if using.

Tip: To toast the coconut, heat a skillet over medium heat. When the pan is hot, add the coconut and cook, stirring frequently, until most of the flakes have turned golden brown, about 4 minutes. Immediately remove the coconut from the hot pan to stop the cooking.

Chocolate-Filled Strawberry Soufflés

MAKES 6 SOUFFLÉS

PER SERVING:

- ▶ CALORIES: 81
- ▶ FAT (GRAMS): 2.1
- ▶ CHOLESTEROL (MILLIGRAMS):3
- ▶ SODIUM (MILLIGRAMS): 45
- ▶ CARBOHYDRATES (GRAMS): 11.5
- ▶ FIBER (GRAMS): 1.5
- ▶ PROTEIN (GRAMS): 3.4

These airy soufflés contain a delicious surprise: A molten center of antioxidant-rich dark chocolate. Strawberries are a fruit with fewer carbohydrates than most, and they are an excellent source of vitamin C, manganese, and cancer-fighting antioxidants.

1 TEASPOON UNSALTED BUTTER, AT ROOM TEMPERATURE

4 CUPS DICED FRESH STRAWBERRIES

¾ CUP NONCALORIC GRANULATED SWEETENER (SUCH AS SPLENDA), PLUS 1 TABLESPOON

1 TABLESPOON CORNSTARCH

1 TEASPOON VANILLA EXTRACT

4 EGG WHITES, AT ROOM TEMPERATURE

¼ TEASPOON CREAM OF TARTAR

½ OUNCE DARK CHOCOLATE, CHOPPED

1. Preheat the oven to 400°F. Position the oven rack in the center. Grease six 4-ounce ramekins with butter and place them on a baking sheet.

2. In a medium saucepan over medium-high heat, bring the strawberries, ¼ cup water, and ¼ cup of the sweetener to a simmer, then turn down the heat to medium-low, stirring frequently.

continued ▶

3. In a small bowl, stir together the cornstarch with 1 tablespoon water until smooth. Pour the cornstarch mixture into the simmering strawberry mixture and cook, stirring until thickened, about 1 minute. Remove from the heat and let cool. Add the vanilla.

4. In a clean large bowl using an electric mixer, beat the egg whites until they become thick. With the mixer running, add the cream of tartar and the remaining ¼ cup of the sweetener, a spoonful at a time, until all of the sweetener has been added and the mixture forms stiff, glossy peaks.

5. Gently fold one-third of the egg white mixture into the strawberry mixture, then fold the strawberry mixture into the remaining egg white mixture, folding gently until fully incorporated.

6. Spoon some of the mixture into the prepared ramekins, filling each about half full.

7. Drop some of the chocolate into the center of each, dividing the chocolate equally. Top each with the remaining soufflé mixture.

8. On the baking sheet, the ramekins should have 2 inches of space between them. Bake until the soufflés are puffed and golden, about 9 minutes. Serve immediately.

Frosted Brownies

MAKES 12 BROWNIES

PER SERVING:

- ▶ CALORIES: 240
- ▶ FAT (GRAMS): 21.3
- ▶ CHOLESTEROL
(MILLIGRAMS): 108

- ▶ SODIUM (MILLIGRAMS): 109
- ▶ CARBOHYDRATES (GRAMS): 8.5
- ▶ FIBER (GRAMS): 3.3
- ▶ PROTEIN (GRAMS): 8.5

Rich, chocolaty, delicious—these are everything you could ask for in a brownie. Moist and dense, they are loaded with deep, dark chocolate flavor (and you get bonus antioxidants, too).

BROWNIES:

COOKING SPRAY

4 OUNCES UNSWEETENED BAKING CHOCOLATE

½ CUP UNSALTED BUTTER

2 CUPS NONCALORIC GRANULATED SWEETENER (SUCH AS SPLENDA)

½ CUP HEAVY CREAM

5 EGGS

1 TABLESPOON VANILLA EXTRACT

1¼ CUPS SOY FLOUR

2 TEASPOONS BAKING POWDER

FROSTING:

3 TABLESPOONS UNSALTED BUTTER, AT ROOM TEMPERATURE

1 CUP NONCALORIC GRANULATED SWEETENER (SUCH AS SPLENDA)

5 TABLESPOONS UNSWEETENED COCOA POWDER

⅓ CUP HEAVY CREAM

1 TEASPOON VANILLA EXTRACT

Preheat the oven to 325°F. Coat an 8-inch square baking pan with cooking spray.

continued ▶

For the Brownies:

1. In the top of a double boiler set over simmering water, melt the chocolate and butter. Add 1 cup of the sweetener and ¼ cup of the cream. Whisk until the mixture is thoroughly combined. Remove from heat.

2. In a large bowl using an electric mixer set on high speed, beat the eggs, the remaining 1 cup of sweetener, and the vanilla until just combined. With the mixer set on low, beat in the chocolate mixture. Stir in the soy flour, baking powder, and the remaining ¼ cup of cream until well combined.

3. Transfer the batter to the prepared baking pan. Bake for about 35 minutes, or until a toothpick inserted into the center comes out clean. Remove from the oven and cool completely in the pan on a wire rack before frosting.

For the Frosting:

1. In a medium bowl using an electric mixer set on medium-high, beat together the butter, sweetener, cocoa, cream, and vanilla until well combined and thick.

2. When the brownies have completely cooled, spread the frosting on top using an offset spatula. Cut the brownies into 12 squares and serve at room temperature.

Ten Tips for Dining Out

Dining out while maintaining your low-carb diet is one of the biggest challenges you will face. It can be difficult to assess exactly what ingredients are in dishes that you see on a menu, so you may not have the slightest idea how many carbs some contain. You can steer clear of obvious carb bombs, like spaghetti or chocolate cake, but sometimes it's hard to find anything listed that is even remotely low-carb. Still, it is possible to eat out without sending your low-carb diet off the rails. Here are ten tips to help you navigate a low-carb diet in a restaurant setting:

1. **Choose your restaurants wisely.** Stay away from noodle joints and bakeries and opt instead for restaurants that serve salads, grilled meats or fish, and other simple foods that tend to come separately rather than in dishes with many ingredients.

2. **Steer clear of fast-food and chain restaurants, where the food is likely to be full of high-carb fillers and sugar.** If you can't avoid going to a fast-food restaurant, check the nutrition information, which should be posted in the restaurant (and might be available on the restaurant's website) to find the best options. Most fast-food restaurants these days have salad options and many offer low-carb wraps instead of bread for burgers and sandwiches. Ask for high-carb condiments like ketchup to be left off or served on the side.

3. **Ask your server questions about how the food is prepared and what goes into the dish.** If the server doesn't know, ask them to check with the chef.

4. **Speak up.** Don't be shy about telling your server that you are on a strict low-carb diet and asking for your food to be prepared without added starch, sugar, or high-carb condiments if at all possible.

5. **Go for something simple,** like grilled or roasted meat or fish (no breading), rather than a complicated curry, braised dish, or casserole that has many ingredients. The more ingredients a dish has, the more likely some of them are high in carbs.

6. **Ask for extra vegetables or salad (without croutons)** in place of potatoes, French fries, pasta, or other high-carb sides.
7. **Ask for burgers to be served with lettuce leaves** for wrapping instead of buns and for sandwich fillings to be served atop salad greens instead of on bread.
8. **Decline the bowl of chips or basket of bread** when it is brought to the table.
9. **Stay away** from breaded or deep-fried foods.
10. **Don't order dessert.** If you simply must have a little something to finish off your meal, order a cup of herbal tea and sweeten it with a sugar-free sweetener, or, if you really can't resist, have one bite of your companion's dessert and be done with it.

High-Carb Foods and Lower-Carb Alternatives

HIGH-CARB FOODS	CARBS PER SERVING (GRAMS)	FIBER PER SERVING (GRAMS)	LOWER CARB ALTERNATIVES	CARBS PER SERVING (GRAMS)	FIBER PER SERVING (GRAMS)
White rice flour	32	1	Flaxseed meal	8	8
White flour	25	1	Hazelnut meal	5	3
			Almond meal	6	3
			Soy flour	8	3
			Coconut flour	16	10
			Buckwheat flour	21	4
White bread	14	0.5	Lettuce leaves	0.5	0
Whole-wheat bread	14	2			
Hamburger bun	21	0			
Flour tortilla	25.3	0			
Whole-wheat tortilla	20	3			
Rice noodles	43.8	1.8	Spaghetti squash	4	1
Spaghetti	42.8	2.5	Zucchini "noodles"	5	2
Whole-wheat spaghetti	37.2	6.3	Shredded, sautéed cabbage	3	2
Long-grain brown rice	44.8	3.5	Cauliflower "rice"	5.3	2.5
Long-grain white rice	44.5	0.6			
French fries	27.2	2.5	Oven-baked zucchini fries	7.1	2.5
Sweet potato fries	22.1	2.5			
Mashed potatoes	35.2	3.1	Puréed cauliflower	5.3	2.5
Honey	17	0	Noncaloric sweeteners	0	0
Maple syrup	13	0			
Granulated sugar	12.6	0			

Low-Carb Foods

Most meats and seafood contain no carbohydrates at all, so they are always a good choice. Just make sure carbs are not added in the preparation method, such as breading or deep frying, or sauces containing sugar or starch. A few exceptions to this are certain shellfish and organ meats, which contain small amounts of carbohydrates per serving.

This chart lists the best low-carb choices for fruits and vegetables. You'll notice that some foods, particularly legumes, may have fairly high carb counts, but they are also high in fiber, making their net carbs more acceptable.

FOOD	SERVING SIZE	CARBS (GRAMS)	FIBER
Apples	½ medium	11	2.5
Bananas	1 small	23	3
Blueberries	½ cup	10.5	1.75
Cherries	½ cup	9.35	1.25
Grapes (red)	½ cup	14	1
Kiwi	1	11.1	2.3
Mangos	½ cup	12	1.5
Peaches	1 small	7.5	1.2
Plums	1 small	3.3	1
Strawberries	½ cup	5.7	1
Acorn squash	½ cup	15	4.5
Asparagus	½ cup	3.7	1.8
Broccoli	½ cup	5.6	2.6
Brussels sprouts	½ cup	6.5	3.2
Butternut squash	½ cup	10.75	3
Carrots	1 medium	5.8	1.7
Cauliflower	½ cup	2.5	1.4
Kale	1 cup	6	6
Lettuce	1 cup	1.8	1.2

FOOD	SERVING SIZE	CARBS (GRAMS)	FIBER
Onions	1 tablespoon	1.5	0.2
Red bell peppers	1 medium	4	1
Swiss chard	1 cup	7.2	3.7
Tomatoes	¼ cup	1.5	1
Black beans	½ cup	20	8
Chickpeas	¼ cup	27	8
Great Northern beans	¼ cup	8.5	3
Kidney beans	¼ cup	10.8	3.9
Lentils	½ cup	17	4.5
Lima beans	½ cup	23	6
Pinto beans	½ cup	18	7
Soy beans	½ cup	13	12

Index

A

almonds
  Fluffy Almond Pancakes with Fresh Berries, 44–45
  Kale and Almond Salad with Parmesan Cheese and Lemon Vinaigrette, 72–73
alternative low-carb foods, 115–116
appetizers and snacks, 51–62
  Bacon-Chile-Cheese Bites with Pecans, 55
  Baked Barbecue Zucchini Chips, 53–54
  Cabbage-Wrapped Fresh Thai Spring Rolls, 57–58
  Cherry and Chocolate Snack Bars, 61–62
  Chocolate Shake, 60
  Crispy Parmesan Kale Chips, 52
  Olive Tapenade–Filled Cucumber Bites, 56
  Orange Cream Ice Pops, 59
artificial sweeteners vs. sugars, 17–18

B

bacon
  Bacon-Chile-Cheese Bites with Pecans, 55
  Seared Trout with Cherry Tomatoes and Bacon, 88–89
Baked Barbecue Zucchini Chips, 53–54
Banana-Chocolate–Peanut Butter "Ice Cream," 98

beef dishes
  Lemon-Rosemary Seared Steak with Asparagus and Mushrooms, 95–96
  Steak Salad with Blue Cheese Dressing, 78–79
blueberries, Honey-Blueberry Tart, 103–104
breakfast recipes, 33–49
  Bacon-Crusted Mini Quiches with Mushrooms and Greens, 38–39
  Crispy Cauliflower Pancakes, 40–41
  Fluffy Almond Pancakes with Fresh Berries, 44–45
  Glazed Cinnamon Roll Muffins, 48–49
  No-Bake Peanut Butter–Coconut Protein Bars, 46–47
  Prosciutto, Spinach, and Cream Baked Eggs, 36–37
  Savory Cottage Cheese Muffins, 42–43
  Spring Pea and Mint Frittata with Goat Cheese and Pancetta, 34–35
Butternut Squash and Chipotle Soup, 64–65

C

Cabbage-Wrapped Fresh Thai Spring Rolls, 57–58
carbs, good vs. bad, 9–10, 17

Carrot Cake with Whipped Coconut Cream Frosting, 107–108
cauliflower
  Crispy Cauliflower Pancakes, 40–41
  Pizza Margherita with a Cauliflower Crust, 82–84
  Roasted Cauliflower Soup with Smoked Gouda, 66–67
Cherry and Chocolate Snack Bars, 61–62
chicken dishes
  Cobb Salad, 76–77
  Creamy Chicken Soup with Roasted Garlic, 70–71
  Prosciutto-Wrapped Chicken Stuffed with Goat Cheese, 93–94
  Seared Chicken Veracruz, 92
chocolate
  Cherry and Chocolate Snack Bars, 61–62
  Chocolate and Vanilla Meringue Swirls, 99–100
  Chocolate Shake, 60
  Chocolate-Filled Strawberry Soufflés, 109–110
Cinnamon-Pecan Thins, 101–102
Cobb Salad, 76–77
cooking tips, 22–23
cottage cheese, Savory Cottage Cheese Muffins, 42–43
cream cheese
  Bacon-Chile-Cheese Bites with Pecans, 55
  Nut-Crusted Mini Maple Cheesecakes, 105–106
Creamy Chicken Soup with Roasted Garlic, 70–71

Crispy Cauliflower
  Pancakes, 40–41
Crispy Parmesan Kale
  Chips, 52
cucumbers, Olive Tapenade–
  Filled Cucumber Bites, 56

D

dessert recipes, 97–112
  Banana-Chocolate–Peanut
    Butter "Ice Cream," 98
  Carrot Cake with Whipped
    Coconut Cream
    Frosting, 107–108
  Chocolate and Vanilla
    Meringue Swirls, 99–100
  Chocolate-Filled
    Strawberry Soufflés,
    109–110
  Cinnamon-Pecan
    Thins, 101–102
  Frosted Brownies, 111–112
  Honey-Blueberry
    Tart, 103–104
  Nut-Crusted Mini Maple
    Cheesecakes, 105–106
dining out tips, 22, 113–114

E

egg dishes
  Bacon-Crusted Mini
    Quiches with
    Mushrooms and
    Greens, 38–39
  Prosciutto, Spinach, and
    Cream Baked Eggs,
    36–37
  Spring Pea and Mint
    Frittata with Goat
    Cheese and
    Pancetta, 34–35
entrée recipes, 81–96
  Garlic-Lime Shrimp
    and Peppers, 87
  Lemon-Rosemary Seared
    Steak with Asparagus
    and Mushrooms,
    95–96
  Pizza Margherita with a
    Cauliflower Crust,
    82–84

Prosciutto-Wrapped
  Chicken Stuffed with
    Goat Cheese, 93–94
  Quinoa and Vegetable
    Gratin, 85–86
  Roasted Salmon with
    Caramelized Leeks,
    90–91
  Seared Chicken Veracruz, 92
  Seared Trout with Cherry
    Tomatoes and Bacon,
    88–89

F

fats, good vs. bad, 18–19
Fluffy Almond Pancakes with
  Fresh Berries, 44–45
Frosted Brownies, 111–112

G

Garlic-Lime Shrimp
  and Peppers, 87
Glazed Cinnamon Roll
  Muffins, 48–49
goat cheese
  Prosciutto-Wrapped
    Chicken Stuffed with
      Goat Cheese, 93–94
  Spring Pea and Mint
    Frittata with Goat
    Cheese and
      Pancetta, 34–35

H

high carb foods, 115–116
Honey-Blueberry
  Tart, 103–104

K

kale
  Crispy Parmesan Kale
    Chips, 52
  Kale and Almond Salad
    with Parmesan Cheese
    and Lemon
      Vinaigrette, 72–73

L

leeks, Roasted Salmon with
  Caramelized Leeks, 90–91
Lemon-Rosemary Seared
  Steak with Asparagus
    and Mushrooms, 95–96
low-carb diets
  cooking tips, 22–23
  dining out tips, 22, 113–114
  good carbs vs. bad
    carbs, 9–10, 17
  health benefits of, 11–12
  myths and misinformation,
    12–15
  preparation tips, 24–26
  recipes for. See recipes
  seven-day meal plans
    for, 27–30. See also
    seven-day meal
    plans shopping tips, 21
low-carb foods, 115–118

M

maple syrup, Nut-Crusted Mini
  Maple Cheesecakes,
    105–106
muffins
  Glazed Cinnamon Roll
    Muffins, 48–49
  Savory Cottage Cheese
    Muffins, 42–43
mushrooms
  Bacon-Crusted Mini
    Quiches with
      Mushrooms and
      Greens, 38–39
  Lemon-Rosemary Seared
    Steak with Asparagus
    and Mushrooms,
      95–96

N

No-Bake Peanut Butter–
  Coconut Protein
    Bars, 46–47
Nut-Crusted Mini Maple
  Cheesecakes, 105–106

O

Olive Tapenade–Filled Cucumber Bites, 56
optimum carb levels, 15–16
Orange Cream Ice Pops, 59

P

pancakes
    Crispy Cauliflower Pancakes, 40–41
    Fluffy Almond Pancakes with Fresh Berries, 44–45
pancetta, Spring Pea and Mint Frittata with Goat Cheese and Pancetta, 34–35
peanut butter
    Banana-Chocolate–Peanut Butter "Ice Cream," 98
    No-Bake Peanut Butter–Coconut Protein Bars, 46–47
pecans
    Bacon-Chile-Cheese Bites with Pecans, 55
    Cinnamon-Pecan Thins, 101–102
Pizza Margherita with a Cauliflower Crust, 82–84
preparation tips, 24–26
prosciutto
    Prosciutto, Spinach, and Cream Baked Eggs, 36–37
    Prosciutto-Wrapped Chicken Stuffed with Goat Cheese, 93–94

Q

Quinoa and Vegetable Gratin, 85–86

R

Radicchio, Fennel, and Orange Salad with Olive Vinaigrette, 74–75

recipes
    appetizers and snacks, 51–62
    breakfasts, 33–49
    desserts, 97–112
    entrées, 81–96
    soups and salads, 63–79
Roasted Cauliflower Soup with Smoked Gouda, 66–67
Roasted Salmon with Caramelized Leeks, 90–91

S

salads, 63, 72–79
    Cobb Salad, 76–77
    Kale and Almond Salad with Parmesan Cheese and Lemon Vinaigrette, 72–73
    Radicchio, Fennel, and Orange Salad with Olive Vinaigrette, 74–75
    Steak Salad with Blue Cheese Dressing, 78–79
salmon, Roasted Salmon with Caramelized Leeks, 90–91
Savory Cottage Cheese Muffins, 42–43
Seared Chicken Veracruz, 92
Seared Trout with Cherry Tomatoes and Bacon, 88–89
seven-day meal plans, 27–30
shopping tips, 21
shrimp, Garlic-Lime Shrimp and Peppers, 87
smoked gouda, Roasted Cauliflower Soup with Smoked Gouda, 66–67
soups, 63–71
    Butternut Squash and Chipotle Soup, 64–65
    Creamy Chicken Soup with Roasted Garlic, 70–71
    Roasted Cauliflower Soup with Smoked Gouda, 66–67

Veggie-Packed Minestrone Soup, 68–69
stocking low-carb kitchens, 21–22
strawberries
    Chocolate-Filled Strawberry Soufflés, 109–110
    Fluffy Almond Pancakes with Fresh Berries, 44–45
sugars vs. artificial sweeteners, 17–18
Swiss chard, Bacon-Crusted Mini Quiches with Mushrooms and Greens, 38–39

T

trout, Seared Trout with Cherry Tomatoes and Bacon, 88–89

V

Veggie-Packed Minestrone Soup, 68–69

W

walnuts, Nut-Crusted Mini Maple Cheesecakes, 105–106
weight-loss mechanisms, 6–11

Y

yogurt, Orange Cream Ice Pops, 59

Z

zucchini, Baked Barbecue Zucchini Chips, 53–54

CPSIA information can be obtained
at www.ICGtesting.com
Printed in the USA
JSHW052148250522
26042JS00002B/2

9 781623 153182